The Complete French Poems of
Rainer Maria Rilke

The Complete French Poems of

RAINER MARIA
RILKE

Translated by A. Poulin, Jr.

Graywolf Press

Publication of this volume is made possible in part by a grant provided by the Minnesota State Arts Board, through an appropriation by the Minnesota State Legislature, a grant from the Wells Fargo Foundation Minnesota, and a grant from the National Endowment for the Arts. Significant support has also been provided by the Bush Foundation; the Lannan Foundation; Marshall Field's Project Imagine with support from the Target Foundation; the McKnight Foundation; and by other generous contributions from foundations, corporations, and individuals. To these organizations and individuals we offer our heartfelt thanks.

MINNESOTA
STATE ARTS BOARD

NATIONAL
ENDOWMENT
FOR THE ARTS

TARGET.

The French poems included in this book were originally collected in Rainer Maria Rilke, *Sämtliche Werke*, Zweiter Band, Gedichte: Zweiter Teil, Insel-Verlag, 1958.

Published by Graywolf Press
250 Third Avenue North, Suite 600
Minneapolis, Minnesota 55401
All rights reserved.

www.graywolfpress.org

Published in the United States of America

ISBN 978-1-55597-361-2

4   6   8   9   7   5   3

Library of Congress Control Number: 2001096555

Cover design: Scott Sorenson
Cover illustration: Don Kilpatrick

FOR

BASILIKE AND DAPHNE

Contents

Foreword

Ever since I first read Rilke's German poems, I knew he had also written poems in French. I assumed though (and many readers must share this misconception) that those were few and slight—like Eliot's French poems, more a language exercise than a serious effort at poetic creation. I am startled, now, to find that they run to nearly 400—enough to establish a significant career even had Rilke written nothing else. The two sequences from that corpus which A. Poulin, Jr. has chosen, here, to translate give warning that the French poems may also carry considerable weight and power.

According to Siegfried Mandel, Rilke had written only 28 French poems before 1922. In that year, of course, he was able to complete the *Duino Elegies,* the massive work that had remained unfinished through 10 years of terrible silence. As is well known, in the great release and outpouring of energy after the completion of his masterpiece, Rilke composed, in 18 days, all 56 of *The Sonnets to Orpheus.* According to Mandel, Rilke composed all of the rest of his French poems between this period and his death in 1926. So we must consider them also, I think, part of that triumphant overflow of celebration and praise; even the choice of the second language seems part of their joyous superfluity of creation. Like the rose in the first of these poems, Rilke had found such repose and sleep in his own center, that his tendernesses could wake, "touch, converge into an urgent mouth."

In both style and subject, also, these poems are closely related to *The Sonnets to Orpheus.* They offer us all of Rilke's accustomed elegance of attitude, his grace of diction, above all his wealth and generosity of creation, that effortless heaping of image upon image, invention upon invention, loveliness upon loveliness. At times they seem so quintessentially Rilkean as to be downright unrepresentative.

And there *are* differences; unquestionably they are lighter, more joyous, more deft and playful. I cannot help wondering how much this coloring may be influenced by the different language; but perhaps it is merely that the fearful confrontation of the abyss has receded further into the past. In any case, these poems lack the muscularity, the monumental awkwardness of the *Elegies,* even of such shorter poems as "Orpheus, Eurydice, Hermes." Merely to mention their generosity is, perhaps, to admit that they are gratuitous, an unforced gift, not under the compulsion of Rilke's most profound creations. They are unnecessary, as were the *airs de cour* of the French Renaissance—small acts of unexacted delight at the accomplishment of an obligatory mission. Like the *airs*, they may seem to slip toward the precious if we forget the past struggle on which they are based.

Having himself faced the trial of translating the *Duino Elegies* and *The Sonnets to Orpheus*, Poulin now turns, as Rilke himself did, to this poetry of bounty. There is an irony, here, however. Translating the *Sonnets* and the *Elegies*, Poulin was forced to sojourn in Rilke's native language, one alien to him. Translating *The Roses* and *The Windows* where Rilke leaves his native language, Poulin is restored to *his*. In any case, he has made available to those of us who read neither, a new and unsuspected wealth of joyous inventions; how could we be less than grateful!

W. D. Snodgrass
Norfolk, Va.
August 12, 1978

Preface

This book is a paperback collection of the five-volume series of books devoted to the French poetry of Rainer Maria Rilke which I have had the privilege to translate and which is being published for the first time in the United States by Graywolf Press.

The first volume in the series, *Saltimbanques* (1978), was a small collection of six French prose poems by Rilke and issued only in a limited edition. The second, with a Foreword by W. D. Snodgrass and issued in a trade edition (as were all others), focused on Rilke's two French sequences, *The Roses & The Windows* (1980). *The Astonishment of Origins* included 14 short sequences, ranging from two to six poems per sequence, the 15-poem sequence entitled "Affectionate Taxes to France," and the 39-poem sequence, "The Valaisian Quatrains." The fourth volume focused exclusively on Rilke's 77-poem sequence, *Orchards,* which includes at least three sub-sequences, "Eros," "Spring," and "Orchard." The fifth volume, *The Migration of Powers,* included most of Rilke's remaining individual French poems, except for a miscellany of occasional verses and "dedications," which are published in this collection for the first time.*

At the close of this long and fruitful labor, we're proud to have offered the first comprehensive collection of Rilke's French poetry in translation, as well as in the original, to appear in the English-speaking world.

That Rilke wrote poems in French is not necessarily important per se; he also happens to have written two poems in Italian. That he wrote such a substantial body of poetry in French, however, is another matter altogether. As W. D. Snodgrass noted in his Foreword to *The Roses & The Windows,* by the end of February 1922, when in less than two months he completed all of the *Duino Elegies* and *The Sonnets to Orpheus,* Rilke had written only a handful of poems in French—28, in fact. By the time of his death in December of 1926, in addition to the many other German poems he'd completed after the *Elegies* and the *Sonnets,* Rilke also had

---

* *The Roses & The Windows* and *Orchards* are Rilke's titles; *Saltimbanques, The Astonishment of Origins,* and *The Migration of Powers* are the translator's titles.

written nearly 400 poems in French—a staggering average of 100 French poems per year! In other words, in only four years Rilke wrote more poems in a language foreign to him than most poets write in their native tongue during an entire lifetime. Such a large body of work by one of this century's greatest poets surely warrants our serious attention, especially when the more we read them the more we realize the extent to which they are an integral part of Rilke's canon and probably have been overlooked by many critics to date.

To say that Rilke's French poems are not his "major" work is to belabor the obvious; many of the poems in *Das Buch der Bilder* and *Neue Gedichte* aren't his "major" work either. Just as obvious is the fact that some of these poems are more successful than others; such is the fickle nature of art, even in the hands of a genius.

In his recent biography, *A Ringing Glass: The Life of Rainer Maria Rilke* (Oxford University Press, 1986), Donald Prater notes that both Valéry and Gide responded generously to Rilke's French poems. "Valéry wrote his admiration for the 'astonishingly delicate strangeness of your French sound . . .'; while Gide found in Rilke's French verse 'a new joy, its quality a little different and more rare perhaps, more delicate, subtler'." Prater further remarks that, although Rilke had attempted to write in French before, "Now [at Muzot] he felt for the first time an impulse to 'active obedience to this admired language,' and the flow continued, in a progression which [Rilke] found positively rejuvenating. . . . He may well have felt too, as Boris Pasternak later surmised, that in German he had reached the very limit of abstraction and was unable to return to those 'details of the beginning without which the artist's word cannot emerge— in French he could become a beginner again'."

Individually and collectively, then, these French poems bear the unmistakable stamp of Rilke's masterful impetus and imagination at the fullness of his maturity. And at the heart of these poems is much the same vision as that found in the *Sonnets* and the *Elegies*: the poetic transformation of the world as a result of intense attentiveness to the things of this world.

⌣

The poems in *The Roses & The Windows* are generally marked by a kind of exuberance and fragility, as well as by an intense inventiveness, heaping image upon image, that's reminiscent of the energy informing *The Sonnets to Orpheus*—but with a greater measure of joyful freedom. Poem XI from "The Roses" is indicative:

All that spinning on your stem
to end yourself, round rose,
doesn't that make you dizzy?
But drenched by your own impetus,

in your bud you just ignore
yourself. It's a world that whirls
around so its calm center dares
the round repose of the round rose.

There isn't that kind of joyfully serious "play" in many poems collected
here. However, there *are* several moments when, for one reason or an-
other, they unmistakably do evoke *The Sonnets to Orpheus*; one example is
the technique in poem 17 from "The Valaisian Quatrains":

Before you can count ten
all changes: the wind takes
the brightness from high
stalks of maize

to throw it on all sides;
it flies, it slides
along a precipice
toward a sister brightness

which, already taken up
in this rough game,
in turn moves herself
toward other altitudes.

And, as if caressed,
dazzled by these games
that maybe gave it shape,
the vast surface rests.

The controlled thrust of that poem's inner rhythm and the manner in
which it is resolved in the last stanza are very similar to those found in
sonnet 23 of the First Series to Orpheus. Meanwhile, the device of using
essentially the same word as a verb and as a noun in the first poem of

"Small Notebook" is also the same as that found in sonnet 13 of the Second Series to Orpheus; in fact, Rilke uses the word "winter" in both poems:

> O you, small heart that winters
> out these bitter winter days with us. . . .
> ("Small Notebook")

> For among winters there's one so endlessly winter
> that, wintering out, your heart will really last.
> (*Sonnets to Orpheus* II, 13)

And the third stanza of poem 2 of "Graves" reflects the unique Rilkean imaginative energy found throughout the Orphic sonnets:

> The avid hornet has to dive
> before it enters the transparent lair
> of leaning flowers; to be their
> dream, we must come rising from below.

However, most of the poems in *The Astonishment of Origins* (as well as in *Orchards* and *The Migration of Powers*) are more quietly "serious" and somber than those in *The Roses & The Windows*; and their tone, though muted and lyrical, is closer to that of the *Duino Elegies* than to *The Sonnets to Orpheus*. Clearly, the thematic and linguistic energy of the opening sequence, "But It Is Purer to Die," is very similar to that of the *Elegies*. Such phrases as "Death is altogether / too much our parent" and "Look at a child's index and thumb—/ so gentle a vise / even bread is astonished" emerge out of the same emotional and imaginative wellspring that generates and controls much of the *Elegies*. The Angel that appears in the second section of this poem is essentially the same as the Angels that appear throughout the *Elegies*: "This amorphous Angel / who, bit by bit, erects himself on the edge / of our sufferings: bright, fatal and forceful." And what could be more quintessentially Rilke (of the *Elegies*) than the concluding lines of this French poem's third section:

> Springs deny themselves, and flowers,
> bruised by inattentive violences,
> deformed by vague inventors

who excite them to the bitter end,
blossom without saying: Everything's afraid
of you: poor killers of abundances!

Admittedly, not all the French poems here are quite so serious, nor do all evoke the *Elegies* quite so directly. Even the three sequences on "Lies," which are thematically related to Rilke's passionate hatred of dolls and masks in the *Elegies* and elsewhere, are much lighter and occasionally edged with a sense of humor that's certainly not present in the famous passage on dolls in the Fourth Elegy. But these are not elegies; they are lyrics, some happier than others, some more melancholy than others. Moreover, at a time when we virtually demand that all poems be "meaningfully serious" (especially when written by "great poets"), some of these lyrics may strike readers as being just too slight in subject matter. A poem like "Belltower's Song" (12 from "The Valaisian Quatrains") is a clear case in point:

BELLTOWER'S SONG

More than a common tower,
I warm myself to ripen my carillon.
Let it be sweet, let it be good
to the Valaisian women.

I share my manna with them
every Sunday, tone by tone;
let my carillon be good
to the Valaisian women.

Let it be good, let it be sweet;
in the hamlets on Saturday night,
let my carillon fall in drops on
the Valaisian women's Valaisian men.

That, from Rilke!? And yet, to dismiss this poem as too trivial is to ignore and to deprive ourselves of the pleasure of discovering the subtle and delicate sexuality of metaphor at work in this small poem, especially in that unexpected turn in the last stanza.

These French lyrics do not directly undertake great subjects and themes. Rather, they are small poems of careful attentiveness to the things of this world, to the common things of this world, and to the elusive states of being in which the world is poetically transformed. And perhaps the manner in which these poems most call to mind the *Elegies* is by implementing in a foreign tongue and with a quiet, gentle craft (when they are most successful) Rilke's grander themes, announced in the noted exhortations of his Ninth Duino Elegy:

> Maybe we're here only to say: *house,*
> *bridge, well, gate, jug, olive tree, window*—
> at most, *pillar, tower*... but to say them, remember,
> oh, to say them in a way that the things themselves
> never dreamed of existing so intensely....

> And these things, whose lives
> are lived in leaving—they understand when you
> praise them.
> Perishing, they turn to us, the most perishable,
> for help.
> They want us to change them completely in our
> invisible hearts,
> oh—forever—into us! Whoever we may finally be!

And the burden, the struggle of the Rilkean hero, who is also the voice of these French poems, is never to forget that charge. For as Rilke says in the first poem of "Memories of Muzot":

> The naive bread, the common tool,
> the intimacy of familiar things—
> who can't leave them for a little
> emptiness where longing grows.

This is not the place for another full-fledged rehearsal of various theories of translation. My primary concern in this project has been to offer poems that are as successful in English as I can render them, while also remaining as faithful as possible to the French originals. At times, for the sake of the English poem, I have diverted from a more literal translation and opted for what seemed to be a more precise temperamental or emotional equivalent of the original phrase or line. And if the English seems quirky, it's because the French seemed quirky too. (I also believe that now and then the poet-translator must rely on the precision of instinctive equivalence.) However, I hope I haven't simply ignored key words on the hubristic premise that Rilke didn't really mean to use them.

Of course, some phrases remain utterly untranslatable. The last line of "The Flower Carrier" (the first poem in the sequence, "The Three Carriers") is a perfect example. The French text, «Ô Légère!» explodes into a veritable bouquet of meanings in this poem's context, ranging from light (as in "not heavy"), fleet, frivolous, slightly improper and fast (as in "a fast woman"), to suggestions of being quick with one's hands, thus also "light-fingered." There simply is no such multifaceted—or, should I say, multi-seeded equivalent in English. I have had to choose another and clearly more limited kind of resonance for the English phrase.

And then there are some poems which, regardless of the translator, just don't work in English—sometimes because they don't work particularly well in the original either—but which must be attempted because they are part of a sequence. "To a Friend" (poem 4 from "Affectionate Taxes to France") may be one of those poems. In fact, even shortly before I submitted this manuscript for final publication, I was tempted to offer only a prose transliteration of the original and invite readers to supply versions of their own. What appears here is my resolution of Rilke's multiple use of the French word *exposé* which is simply *de trop* in English.

No doubt the translator's greatest challenge—especially when dealing with this kind of formal French poetry—is to reconstruct the original French music in English, without inordinate inversions that risk casting the English into the syncopated singsong of a nursery rhyme, especially if one wishes to remain relatively faithful to the original words and meanings. Perhaps the poet-translator is one of the people in the world who most acutely realizes why music is the queen of the arts: the French virtuoso never has to "translate" the Russian composer's sonata into French before performing it! But perhaps soon a more adept poet-translator (who might also be a musician?) will be able to go far beyond my occasional and approximate rhymes, my modified cadences, and reproduce Rilke's original French music far more accurately than I have done.

A few comments on the texts are necessary. To begin with, the arrangement of the sequences in these books is neither Rilke's nor is it in chronological order according to dates of composition. Rather, the arrangement of the sequences here is my own.

The somewhat strange title of the sequence, "Affectionate Taxes to France," no doubt results from the fact that Rilke lived in France for many years but was never a citizen of that country. (Somehow, "tender" or even "overdue" taxes to France didn't reflect the spirit of the original.) Poem 8 (except for the last stanza), as well as poems 10 and 11 in this sequence, also appear in Rilke's other French sequence, *Vergers (Orchards)*.

During the last years of his life, Rilke lived in the village of Muzot (prounounced Mu-zótte), which is located in the Swiss canton of Valais in the Rhône Valley. Thus the title of the sequence, "The Valaisian Quatrains." The last three poems in "The Valaisian Quatrains" are not part of Rilke's original sequence; they appear among his many other miscellaneous French poems. However, since Rilke clearly identified them as "Other Valaisian Quatrains," I have included them as part of this sequence in translation.

While I've adhered strictly to the French texts as they appear in what is to date the definitive edition of Rilke's work published by Insel-Verlag, I have taken the liberty of eliminating certain parentheses, around essentially grammatical words, that Rilke either forgot or chose to omit in his original text. I also have corrected one or two very basic spelling errors, and have attempted to make the punctuation and capitalization throughout the sequences somewhat more consistent.

One lives with projects such as these for so long that after a while one also fails to notice even the most stupid of errors, never mind the more subtle dimensions of language and of poetry. Thus, I am most grateful to my editor, Scott Walker, and to Helen Byers for having read intermediate versions of these translations and made suggestions for their improvement. Many of these translations' felicities are the result of those good people's generosity. The limitations are entirely mine.

[Adapted from the Preface to
THE ASTONISHMENT OF ORIGINS]

A. Poulin, Jr.
Brockport, N.Y.
July 3, 1986

Les Roses

The Roses

This translation for
BERTRAND MATHIEU

Rose, ô pure contradiction,
volupté de n'être le sommeil de personne
sous tant de paupières.
—R. M. RILKE

I

Si ta fraîcheur parfois nous étonne tant,
heureuse rose,
c'est qu'en toi-même, en dedans,
pétale contre pétale, tu te reposes.

Ensemble tout éveillé, dont le milieu
dort, pendant qu'innombrables, se touchent
les tendresses de ce cœur silencieux
qui aboutissent à l'extrême bouche.

II

Je te vois, rose, livre entrebâillé,
qui contient tant de pages
de bonheur détaillé
qu'on ne lira jamais. Livre-mage,

qui s'ouvre au vent et qui peut être lu
les yeux fermés . . .
dont les papillons sortent confus
d'avoir eu les mêmes idées.

III

Rose, toi, ô chose par excellence complète
qui se contient infiniment
et qui infiniment se répand, ô tête
d'un corps par trop de douceur absent,

rien ne te vaut, ô toi, suprême essence
de ce flottant séjour;
de cet espace d'amour où à peine l'on avance
ton parfum fait le tour.

I

If we're sometimes so amazed
by your freshness, happy rose,
it's that deep inside yourself,
petal against petal, you're in repose.

Fully awake while their center's slept
who knows how long, this silent
heart's tendernesses touch,
converge into an urgent mouth.

II

I see you, rose, half-open book
filled with so many pages
of that detailed happiness
we will never read. Magus-book,

opened by the wind and read
with our eyes closed . . .
butterflies fly out of you, stunned
for having had the same ideas.

III

Rose, O you completely perfect thing,
always self-contained and yet
spilling yourself forever—O head
of a torso with too much sweetness missing,

nothing's your equal, O you, supreme
essence of this fragile place;
your perfume is the very seam
of this love-space we barely penetrate.

IV

C'est pourtant nous qui t'avons proposé
de remplir ton calice.
Enchantée de cet artifice,
ton abondance l'avait osé.

Tu étais assez riche, pour devenir cent fois toi-même
en une seule fleur;
c'est l'état de celui qui aime. . . .
Mais tu n'as pas pensé ailleurs.

V

Abandon entouré d'abandon,
tendresse touchant aux tendresses. . . .
C'est ton intérieur qui sans cesse
se caresse, dirait-on . . .

se caresse en soi-même,
par son propre reflet éclairé.
Ainsi tu inventes le thème
du Narcisse exaucé.

VI

Une rose seule, c'est toutes les roses
et celle-ci: l'irremplaçable,
le parfait, le souple vocable
encadré par le texte des choses.

Comment jamais dire sans elle
ce que furent nos espérances,
et les tendres intermittences
dans la partance continuelle.

IV

Surely it was us who encouraged
you to refill your calyx.
Enchanted by such artifice,
your abundance found its courage.

You were rich enough to be yourself
a hundred times in just one flower;
that's the condition of the lover. . . .
But you never did think otherwise.

V

Abandon surrounds abandon,
tenderness touches tenderness. . . .
You'd think your center would caress
itself on and on and on . . .

caress itself in itself and seem
to glow with its own image.
Thus you invent the theme
of the fulfilled Narcissus.

VI

A single rose is every rose
and this one: irreplaceable,
perfect, a supple vocable
by the text of things enclosed.

Without her, how can we ever
talk about what our hopes were,
about the tender intervals
in this perpetual departure.

VII

T'appuyant, fraîche claire
rose, contre mon œil fermé—
on dirait mille paupières
superposées

contre la mienne chaude.
Mille sommeils contre ma feinte
sous laquelle je rôde
dans l'odorant labyrinthe.

VIII

De ton rêve trop plein,
fleur en dedans nombreuse,
mouillée comme une pleureuse,
tu te penches sur le matin.

Tes douces forces qui dorment,
dans un désir incertain,
développent ces tendres formes
entre joues et seins.

IX

Rose, toute ardente et pourtant claire,
que l'on devrait nommer reliquaire
de Sainte-Rose ... rose qui distribue
cette troublante odeur de sainte nue.

Rose plus jamais tentée, déconcertante
de son interne paix; ultime amante,
si loin d'Ève, de sa première alerte—
rose qui infiniment possède la perte.

VII

Bright cool rose leaning
on my eye that's closed—
like a thousand eyelids
superimposed

on mine that's warm.
A thousand sleeps against
this counterfeit in which I roam
in a fragrant labyrinth.

VIII

Overflowing with your dream,
flower with so many others deep
inside, wet as one who weeps,
you lean against the dawn.

In a precarious wish,
your gentle sleeping powers
shape those very tender
forms of cheeks and breasts.

IX

Rose, so clear and yet so fiery
that we should call you reliquary
of Saint Rose . . . rose, you dispense
this troubling odor of a naked saint.

Rose never tempted again, disconcerter
by your inner peace; ultimate lover,
so far from Eve, from her first call—
rose infinitely holding the fall.

X

Amie des heures où aucun être ne reste,
où tout se refuse au cœur amer;
consolatrice dont la présence atteste
tant de caresses qui flottent dans l'air.

Si l'on renonce à vivre, si l'on renie
ce qui était et ce qui peut arriver,
pense-t-on jamais assez à l'insistante amie
qui à côté de nous fait son œuvre de fée.

XI

J'ai une telle conscience de ton
être, rose complète,
que mon consentement te confond
avec mon cœur en fête.

Je te respire comme si tu étais,
rose, toute la vie,
et je me sens l'ami parfait
d'une telle amie.

XII

Contre qui, rose,
avez-vous adopté
ces épines?
Votre joie trop fine
vous a-t-elle forcée
de devenir cette chose
armée?

Mais de qui vous protège
cette arme exagérée?
Combien d'ennemis vous ai-je

X

Friend of hours when no one remains,
when all's refused to the bitter heart;
comforter whose presence attests
to such caresses floating in the air.

If we refuse to live, if we renounce
what was and what may happen still,
we never think enough of this tenacious friend
who's next to us, at work on miracles.

XI

I'm so conscious of your being,
total rose,
my assent's confusing
you with my celebrating heart.

Rose, I breathe you in as if
you were all of life,
and I feel I am the perfect
friend of such a friend.

XII

Rose, against whom
did you assume
those thorns?
Did your too delicate
joy force you
to become that
armed thing?

But from whom does this
extravagant weapon protect
you? How many enemies

enlevés
qui ne la craignaient point?
Au contraire, d'été en automne,
vous blessez les soins
qu'on vous donne.

XIII

Préfères-tu, rose, être l'ardente compagne
de nos transports présents?
Est-ce le souvenir qui davantage te gagne
lorsqu'un bonheur se reprend?

Tant de fois je t'ai vue, heureuse et sèche,
—chaque pétale un linceul—
dans un coffret odorant, à côté d'une mèche,
ou dans un livre aimé qu'on relira seul.

XIV

Été: être pour quelques jours
le contemporain des roses;
respirer ce qui flotte autour
de leurs âmes écloses.

Faire de chacune qui se meurt
une confidante,
et survivre à cette sœur
en d'autres roses absente.

XV

Seule, ô abondante fleur,
tu crées ton propre espace;
tu te mires dans une glace
d'odeur.

stole off with you
because they weren't afraid of it?
Instead, from summer to autumn,
you wound the attention
that's poured over you.

XIII

Rose, do you prefer to be the ardent friend
of our present ecstasy?
Or are you won over more by memory,
when one joy's relived again?

How often I have seen you, happy, parched
—each petal a shroud—
in a fragrant box, next to a match,
or in a favorite book re-read alone out loud.

XIV

Summer: for a few days being
the contemporary of roses;
to breathe what's floating
around their hearts in bloom.

To make each dying one
a confidante,
and to survive this sister in
other roses that are absent.

XV

All alone, O abundant flower,
you create your own space;
you stare at yourself in a mirror
of odor.

Ton parfum entoure comme d'autres pétales
ton innombrable calice.
Je te retiens, tu t'étales,
prodigieuse actrice.

XVI

Ne parlons pas de toi. Tu es ineffable
selon ta nature.
D'autres fleurs ornent la table
que tu transfigures.

On te met dans un simple vase—
voici que tout change:
c'est peut-être la même phrase,
mais chantée par un ange.

XVII

C'est toi qui prépares en toi
plus que toi, ton ultime essence.
Ce qui sort de toi, ce troublant émoi,
c'est ta danse.

Chaque pétale consent
et fait dans le vent
quelques pas odorants
invisibles.

Ô musique des yeux!
Toute entourée d'eux,
tu deviens au milieu
intangible.

Your fragrance swirls: more petals
around your teeming calyx.
I hold you back, you sprawl,
marvelous actress.

XVI

Let's not speak of you. Ineffable.
That is your nature.
Other flowers decorate the table
you transfigure.

We put you in a simple vase—
everything is mutable:
perhaps it's the same phrase,
but now sung by an angel.

XVII

It's you who in you is preparing
more than you: your ultimate essence.
The troubling motion emerging
out of you is your dance.

Each petal consents
and takes a few fragrant,
invisible
steps in the wind.

O music of eyes!
Completely circumscribed
by them, in their middle
you become intangible.

XVIII

Tout ce qui nous émeut, tu le partages.
Mais ce qui t'arrive, nous l'ignorons.
Il faudrait être cent papillons
pour lire toutes tes pages.

Il y en a d'entre vous qui sont comme des dictionnaires;
ceux qui les cueillent
ont envie de faire relier toutes ces feuilles.
Moi, j'aime les roses épistolaires.

XIX

Est-ce en exemple que tu te proposes?
Peut-on se remplir comme les roses,
en multipliant sa subtile matière
qu'on avait faite pour ne rien faire?

Car ce n'est pas travailler que d'être
une rose, dirait-on.
Dieu, en regardant par la fenêtre,
fait la maison.

XX

Dis-moi, rose, d'où vient
qu'en toi-même enclose,
ta lente essence impose
à cet espace en prose
tous ces transports aériens?

Combien de fois cet air
prétend que les choses le trouent,
ou, avec une moue,

XVIII

You're touched by all that touches us.
But whatever happens to you we ignore.
We'd have to be a hundred butterflies
to read all those pages of yours.

Some of you are like dictionaries;
people who are their collectors
have an urge to re-read all the entries.
I love roses that are letters.

XIX

Do you set yourself up as example?
Can we replenish our own subtle
matter like roses by multiplying
what we once did just to do nothing?

Because it really isn't work, you know,
just to be a rose.
God, while looking out a window,
picks up the house.

XX

Except from your inner circle, tell me, rose,
where does your slow essence
come from to impose
all those unearthly raptures
on this space of prose?

How often does this air
pretend that everything tears
it, or, with a scowl,

il se montre amer.
Tandis qu'autour de ta chair,
rose, il fait la roue.

XXI

Cela ne te donne-t-il pas le vertige
de tourner autour de toi sur ta tige
pour te terminer, rose ronde?
Mais quand ton propre élan t'inonde,

tu t'ignores dans ton bouton.
C'est un monde qui tourne en rond
pour que son calme centre ose
le rond repos de la ronde rose.

XXII

Vous encore, vous sortez
de la terre des morts,
rose, vous qui portez
vers un jour tout en or

ce bonheur convaincu.
L'autorisent-ils, eux
dont la crâne creux
n'en a jamais tant su?

XXIII

Rose, venue très tard, que les nuits amères arrêtent
par leur trop sidérale clarté,
rose, devines-tu les faciles délices complètes
de tes sœurs d'été?

seems to be so bitter.
While around your petals,
rose, it swaggers.

XXI

All that spinning on your stem
to end yourself, round rose,
doesn't that make you dizzy?
But drenched by your own impetus,

in your bud you just ignore
yourself. It's a world that whirls
around so its calm center dares
the round repose of the round rose.

XXII

You again, you rising
out of the earth of the dead,
rose, you who are carrying
toward a day all in gold

this convincing happiness.
And those whose sunken
skulls have never known
so much, do they say yes?

XXIII

Late-blooming rose that the bitter
nights stop with their too sidereal light,
rose, do you suspect the easy full delights
of your summer sisters?

Pendant des jours et des jours je te vois qui hésites
dans ta gaine serrée trop fort.
Rose qui, en naissant, à rebours imites
les lenteurs de la mort.

Ton innombrable état te fait-il connaître,
dans un mélange où tout se confond,
cet ineffable accord du néant et de l'être
que nous ignorons?

XXIV

Rose, terrestre pourtant, à nous autres égale,
fleur de toutes nos fleurs,
est-ce que tu sens en toi, pétale contre pétale,
nos palpables bonheurs?

Ces attouchements doux qui te remplissent, ô rose,
est-ce que leur somme comprend
tout ce qu'on avait osé, tout ce que l'on ose
et le plaisir hésitant?

XXV

Rose, à nos habitudes si chère,
à nos plus chers souvenirs dédiée,
devenue presque imaginaire
pour être tant à nos rêves liée—

rose qui, silencieuse, surpasse
en se mêlant à l'air, les chants,
qui triomphe dans la rosace
et qui meurt entre deux amants.

Day after day I watch you hesitate
in your sheath too tightly tied.
Rose who, being born, in reverse imitates
the slow ways of those who've died.

Does your endless state make you capable of knowing,
in some *mélange* where everything is fused,
that speechless harmony of nothingness and being
we so ignorantly refuse?

XXIV

Rose, certainly earthly and our equal,
flower of all our flowers,
inside yourself, petal over petal, do you feel
our own palpable pleasures?

These tender touches filling you, O rose,
does their measure comprise
all that we've dared, all that we venture,
and this hesitant happiness?

XXV

Rose, so cherished by our customs,
dedicated to our dearest memories,
become almost imaginary
for being so linked to our dreams—

silent while becoming air, rose
eclipsing all the canticles,
that is triumphant in the rose
window, and between two lovers dies.

XXVI

Infiniment rassurée
malgré tant de dangers
sans jamais rien changer
à ses habitudes,
la rose qui s'ouvre, prélude
à son innombrable durée.

Sait-on combien elle vit?
Un de ses jours, sans doute,
c'est toute la terre, toute
l'infinité d'ici.

XXVII

Rose, eût-il fallu te laisser dehors,
chère exquise?
Que fait une rose là où le sort
sur nous s'épuise?

Point de retour. Te voici
qui partages
avec nous, éperdue, cette vie, cette vie
qui n'est pas de ton âge.

XXVI

Infinitely at ease
despite so many risks,
with no variation
of her usual routine,
the blooming rose is the omen
of her immeasurable endurance.

Do we know how she survives?   ·
No doubt one of her days
is all the earth and all
of our infinity.

XXVII

Rose, did you have to be left
outdoors, exquisite dear?
What is a rose doing here
where fate exhausts itself on us?

Point of no return. You're left
with us now, sharing,
desperately, this life, this life
where you don't belong.

Les Fenêtres

The Windows

for

KIMON FRIAR

Ce qui me reste, c'est . . .
ma joie toujours impénitente
d'avoir aimé des choses ressemblantes
à ces absences qui nous font agir.
　　　　　　　　—R. M. RILKE

I

Il suffit que, sur un balcon
ou dans l'encadrement d'une fenêtre,
une femme hésite... pour être
celle que nous perdons
en l'ayant vue apparaître.

Et si elle lève les bras
pour nouer ses cheveux, tendre vase:
combien notre perte par là
gagne soudain d'emphase
et notre malheur d'éclat!

II

Tu me proposes, fenêtre étrange, d'attendre;
déjà presque bouge ton rideau beige.
Devrais-je, ô fenêtre, à ton invite me rendre?
Ou me défendre, fenêtre? Qui attendrais-je?

Ne suis-je intact, avec cette vie qui écoute,
avec ce cœur tout plein que la perte complète?
Avec cette route qui passe devant, et le doute
que tu puisses donner ce trop dont le rêve m'arrête?

III

N'es-tu pas notre géométrie,
fenêtre, très simple forme
qui sans effort circonscris
notre vie énorme?

Celle qu'on aime n'est jamais plus belle
que lorsqu'on la voit apparaître
encadrée de toi; c'est, ô fenêtre,
que tu la rends presque éternelle.

I

It's enough that on a balcony
or in a window frame
a woman pauses . . . to be
the one we lose
just by seeing her appear.

And if she lifts her arms
to tie her hair, tender vase:
how much our loss gains
a sudden emphasis,
our sadness brilliance!

II

You propose I wait, strange window;
your beige curtain nearly billows.
O window, should I accept your offer or,
window, defend myself? Who would I wait for?

Aren't I intact, with this life that's listening,
with this full heart that loss is completing?
With this road running in front, and the qualm
you give this excess that stops me with its dream?

III

Aren't you our geometry,
window, very simple shape
circumscribing our enormous
life painlessly?

A lover's never so beautiful
as when we see her appear
framed by you; because, window,
you make her almost immortal.

Tous les hasards sont abolis. L'être
se tient au milieu de l'amour,
avec ce peu d'espace autour
dont on est maître.

IV

Fenêtre, toi, ô mesure d'attente,
tant de fois remplie,
quand une vie se verse et s'impatiente
vers une autre vie.

Toi qui sépares et qui attires,
changeante comme la mer—
glace, soudain, oú notre figure se mire
mêlée à ce qu'on voit à travers;

échantillon d'une liberté compromise
par la présence du sort;
prise par laquelle parmi nous s'égalise
le grand trop du dehors.

V

Comme tu ajoutes à tout,
fenêtre, le sens de nos rites:
quelqu'un qui ne serait que debout,
dans ton cadre attend ou médite.

Tel distrait, tel paresseux
—c'est toi qui le mets en page:
il se ressemble un peu,
il devient son image.

Perdu dans un vague ennui,
l'enfant s'y appuie et reste;

All risks are cancelled. Being
stands at love's center,
with this narrow space around,
where we are master.

IV

You, window, O waiting's measure,
refilled so often,
when one life spills out and grows
impatient for another.

You who divides and attracts,
as fickle as the sea—
sudden mirror reflecting our face
mingled with what we see in back;

fraction of a freedom compromised
by the presence of risk;
trapped by whatever's in us
that evens the odds of the loaded outside.

V

Window, how you add the sense
of our rites to everything:
someone who is simply standing
waits or meditates inside your frame.

The one who's lazy or distracted
—you set him into motion:
he looks a little like himself,
he becomes his own reflection.

Lost in vague boredom,
a child leans on you and rests;

il rêve. . . . Ce n'est pas lui,
c'est le temps qui use sa veste.

Et les amantes, les y voit-on,
immobiles et frêles:
percées comme les papillons
pour la beauté de leurs ailes.

VI

Du fond de la chambre, du lit, ce n'était que pâleur qui sépare
    la fenêtre stellaire cédant à la fenêtre avare
        qui proclame le jour.
Mais la voici qui accourt, qui se penche, qui reste:
après l'abandon de la nuit, cette neuve jeunesse céleste
        consent à son tour!

Rien dans le ciel matinal que la tendre amante contemple,
    rien que lui-même, ce ciel, immense exemple:
        profondeur et hauteur!
Sauf les colombes qui font dans l'air de rondes arènes,
où leur vol allumé en douces courbes promène
        un retour de douceur.

VII

Fenêtre, qu'on cherche souvent
pour ajouter à la chambre comptée
tous les grands nombres indomptés
que la nuit va multipliant.

Fenêtre, où autrefois était assise
celle qui, en guise de tendresse,
faisait un lent travail qui baisse
et immobilise. . . .

he dreams. . . . It's not him,
it's time using his vest.

And look at all the loving,
motionless and fragile:
butterflies pinned
for their beautiful wings.

VI

From the back of the room, the bed, only a pallor spread,
     the starry window surrendering to the greedy window
          announcing the day.
But here comes the one who hurries, who leans, and stays:
after night's abandonment, it's this new and heavenly
          girl's turn to say yes!

At nothing else in the morning sky, the tender lover stares
     at nothing but the enormous example of the sky himself:
          the heights and depths!
Only doves making round arenas in the air,
where their flight flashing in soft arcs parades
          a return of gentleness.

VII

Window we so often look for
to add to the calculated room
all the wild high numbers
night will multiply.

Window where once, disguised
as tenderness, a woman
sat doing a slow job
that debased, immobilized. . . .

Fenêtre, dont une image bue
dans la claire carafe germe.
Boucle qui ferme
la vaste ceinture de notre vue.

VIII

Elle passe des heures émues
appuyée à sa fenêtre,
toute au bord de son être,
distraite et tendue.

Comme les lévriers en
se couchant leurs pattes disposent,
son instinct de rêve surprend
et règle ces belles choses

que sont ses mains bien placées.
C'est par là que le reste s'enrôle.
Ni les bras, ni les seins, ni l'épaule,
ni elle-même ne disent: assez!

IX

Sanglot, sanglot, pur sanglot!
Fenêtre, où nul ne s'appuie!
Inconsolable enclos,
plein de ma pluie!

C'est le trop tard, le trop tôt
qui de tes formes décident:
tu les habilles, rideau,
robe du vide!

Window where an image sipped
from the clear carafe grows.
Buckle that can close
the vast circle of our sight.

VIII

She spends anxious hours
leaning on her windowsill,
tense and distracted,
on the edge of her soul.

Like greyhounds arranging
their legs as they lie down,
her dreaming instinct conquers
and rules these beautiful things

that are her well-placed hands.
That's when the rest enlists.
Neither arms, nor shoulders, nor breasts,
nor her very self can say: enough!

IX

Sigh, sigh, pure sigh!
Sill where no one leans!
Inconsolable space
full of my rain!

Your shape determines
what's too soon or too late:
you dress them up, curtain,
vestment of the void!

X

C'est pour t'avoir vue
penchée à la fenêtre ultime,
que j'ai compris, que j'ai bu
tout mon abîme.

En me montrant tes bras
tendus vers la nuit,
tu as fait que, depuis,
ce qui en moi te quitta,
me quitte, me fuit. . . .

Ton geste, fut-il la preuve
d'un adieu si grand,
qu'il me changea en vent,
qu'il me versa dans le fleuve?

XI

Assiette verticale qui nous sert
la pitance qui nous poursuit,
et la trop douce nuit
et le jour, souvent trop amer.

L'interminable repas,
assaisonné de bleu—
il ne faut pas être las
et se nourrir par les yeux.

Que de mets l'on nous propose
pendant que mûrissent les prunes;
ô mes yeux, mangeurs de roses,
vous allez boire la lune!

X

It's because I saw you
leaning out the ultimate
window that I knew
and drank my whole abyss.

Showing me your arms
stretched toward night,
you made what was in
me that escaped you escape
me, since, and run. . . .

Was your one gesture
proof of a goodbye so grand
that it turned me into wind
and dropped me in the river?

XI

Vertical plate serving us
the pittance that pursues
us, the night too tender
and day too often bitter.

Endless meal,
seasoned with blue—
we just can't loll
and let our eyes feed us.

What menus are proposed
during the ripening of prunes;
O my eyes, devourers of roses,
you will drink the moon!

XII

Ce jour je suis d'humeur fenestrière,
rien que de regarder me semble vivre.
Tout me surprend d'un goût complémentaire,
d'intelligence plein comme dans un livre.

Chaque oiseau qui de son vol traverse
mon étendue, veut que je consente.
Et je consens. La force inconstante
ne m'épouvante plus, car elle me berce.

Me trouvera-t-on lorsque la nuit abonde
ayant passé le jour entier peut-être
livré à toi, inépuisable fenêtre,
pour être l'autre moitié du monde.

XIII

Ce jour elle fut d'humeur fenestrière:
rien que de regarder lui semblait vivre.
Elle vit venir, d'inexistence ivre,
un monde à son cœur complémentaire.

On aurait dit que son regard arrose
abondamment un doux jardin d'images;
était-ce liberté ou esclavage
de ne pas changer l'indolente pose?

Son cœur, loin de ce qui vit et vire,
semblait un nombre qui soudain s'éclaire
pareil à la Balance ou la Lyre;
un presque-nom d'absences millénaires.

XII

Today I'm in a window mood,
to live seems just to look,
astonished by the better taste
of all, the fuller insight of a book.

Every bird that flies within
my reach wants me to consent.
I consent. Such an inconstant
force doesn't surprise me now, it soothes.

And when night falls, who knows,
perhaps I'll find I've spent all day
given to you, inexhaustible window,
to be the other half of the world.

XIII

She was in a window mood that day:
to live seemed no more than to stare.
From a dizzy non-existence she could see
a world coming to her completing heart.

She seemed to be profusely watering
a garden of tender images with her glance;
is it liberty or slavery
not to change the pose of indolence?

Far from what's living and spinning, her heart
was a number struck by sudden brilliance
like a Balance or a Lyre;
an almost-name from ancient absences.

XIV

D'abord, au matin, petite fenêtre farouche,
au cinquième, tu te fais presque bouche,
et tu montres usées et exsangues
toutes les langues de la chambre. Ces langues
que notre vain va-et-vient fane et ronge
comme si nous étions leurs grands mensonges.
Aussi on les bat, ces langues, on les punit
de nous avoir dits et toujours redits:
Ô très-indécente descente de lit!

XV

Depuis quand nous te jouons
avec nos yeux, fenêtre!
Comme la lyre, tu devais être
rendue aux constellations!

Instrument tendre et fort
de nos âmes successives,
arrache enfin de nos sorts
ta forme définitive!

Monte! Tourne de loin
autour de nous qui te fîmes.
Soyez, astres, les rimes
trouvées à nos bouts de destin!

XIV

Tiny untamed window on the fifth,
right at dawn you turn into a mouth
of sorts, revealing all your room's
bloodless, battered tongues, tongues our
vain comings-and-goings toss and devour
as if we were their enormous lies.
We also beat these tongues, we chastise
them for having said and said and said:
Oh, how obscene that scene of falling into bed!

XV

Window, just how long have we
played you with our eyes!
Like the lyre, you should be
one of the constellations!

Tender and strong instrument
of our successive souls,
tear out your permanent
form at last from our fates!

Climb! And from afar
spin around us who created you.
Be the rhyme, O star,
found at the end of our end!

Suites Brèves

Short Sequences

for

ARCHIBALD MACLEISH
on his 90th birthday

. . . la vie, à nous, se passe en prélude,
mais parfois le chant qui nous surprend
nous appartient, comme à son instrument.
—R. M. RILKE

«*Mais Il Est Plus Pur de Mourir*»

> Mais il est plus pur de mourir.
> —*Comtesse de Noailles*

1

Tout cela pourrait changer: jamais plus
ce regard que les choses intimes
aiment.... Ce qui arrive, le pourrais-tu
faire? Ce qui tombe par soi-même,
le pourrais-tu jeter? Mon héréditaire
main? Dis! Tu connais la colère—
tu trembles souvent pour être après
d'un calme étrange qui m'inquiète....
Est-ce moi qui t'arrête? Tu sais
caresser.... Mais dans la caresse,
ce trop de douceur qui dans l'autre s'enfonce
n'est-ce point du meurtre déjà qui sans cesse
renonce? Il n'y a qu'une vitre qui nous sépare,
à peine, de la rapide méprise soudaine
du pharmacien qui verse l'abîme,
de l'énorme dépense avare
du crime. Elle est par trop
notre parente, la mort. Le flot
de la vie qui s'accélère,
c'est déjà elle: la mort-mère.

Vois l'index de l'enfant et son pouce—
cette tenaille si douce
que même le pain s'en étonne.
Cette main, toute bonne,
a peut-être tué l'oiseau
et frissonne
de son ultime sursaut.
Sa brusque négation de fouine
qui l'empêcherait, qui l'empêche?

Il y a une brèche
dans notre cœur en ruine.

"But It Is Purer to Die"

> But it is purer to die
> —*Comtesse de Noailles*

1

All that could change: never again
this look that intimate things
love. . . . Whatever happens, could you
cause it? Whatever falls by itself,
could you throw it? My hereditary
hand? Speak! You know anger—
you often tremble, later becoming
a strange calm that worries me. . . .
Is it I who stops you? You know
how to caress. . . . But in the caress,
that excess gentleness that sinks into the other,
isn't there already murder that forever
denies? No more than a windowpane
separates us from the sudden rapid scorn
of the chemist pouring the abyss,
of crime's enormous selfish
waste. Death is altogether
too much our parent. The flow
of life that accelerates
is already her: mother-death.

Look at a child's index and thumb—
so gentle a vise
even bread is astonished.
Utterly good, perhaps
that hand has killed a bird
and trembles
with its final spasm.
Its quick, weasel-like denial
that would stop it, who stops it?

There is a gap
in our ruined heart.

2

N'osez pas les nommer! De Demi-Dieux à peine
à notre bouche obscure sont permis. . . .
Et l'âme même d'insistance pleine
ne connaît que cet Ange indécis
qui peu à peu s'érige sur le bord
de nos souffrances: clair, fatal et fort,
ne défaillant jamais et sans vertige,
mais malgré tout, lui-même, être-lige
d'un inconnu et souverain accord.

Lui, Majuscule, Lettre verticale
du mot que, lentement, nous défaisons;
borne d'airain de notre vie natale,
mesure anonyme de ces monts
qui forment une chaîne dans le cœur
en sa partie abrupte et sauvage. . . .
Statue du port, phare de l'abordage,
et, pourtant, des naufrages contempteur!

Vivre par lui, c'est notre but ultime,
entre l'enfance lente et le crime,
vivre par lui dans un élan si vrai,
que sa rigueur de roche qui se tait
finit par changer de silence . . . pour
taire un consentement. . . .

3

Renoncez, pieux clients! Les cierges allumés
n'ont plus le pouvoir de remuer les ombres
dans ces visages peints et rajustés qu'encombre
l'indifférent vernis de vétusté.
Reconcez doucement à demander l'avis
de ces partants que la prière offusque;

2

Do not dare name them! Half-Gods
hardly are allowed in our dark mouths. . . .
And, even full of insistence, the soul
knows only this amorphous Angel
who, bit by bit, erects himself on the edge
of our sufferings: bright, fatal and forceful,
never flinching, never afraid of heights,
but for all that, himself the vassal-being
of an unknown and sovereign contract.

Him, Capital, vertical Letter
of the word that, slowly, we demolish;
brass boundary of our native life,
anonymous measure of those mountains
forming a chain in our heart,
in its abrupt and savage part. . . .
Harbor statue, landing beacon,
and yet, contemptuous shipwrecks!

Between slow childhood and the crime,
our final goal is to live in him,
to live in him in so true an impulse
that, silencing itself, his rock-rigor
ends up being changed by silence . . .
to silence an agreement. . . .

3

Pious clients, give up! Those lighted candles
are no longer powerful enough to move the shadows
on those painted, readjusted faces
burdened by the indifferent varnish of decay.
Softly give up asking the advice
of the departed dazzled by prayer;

il leur a bien fallu des cœurs plus brusques
pour être de leurs cris ravis.

Renoncez à ce marchandage doux.

Mais en vous-mêmes, tout au fond de vous,
quel cimetière! Que de Dieux absous,
congédiés, oubliés, hors d'usage,
que de prophètes, que de mages
abandonnés par votre désir fou!

Vous avez dépeuplé les cieux immenses.
Et les dryades privées de leur chance,
sont rentrées dans les arbres et n'avancent
que dans la sève, versant pleurs et pleurs. . . .
Les sources se renient, et les fleurs
brisées par de distraites violences,
déformées par de vagues inventeurs
qui les excitent à outrance,
fleurissent sans se dire. . . . Tout a peur
de vous: pauvres tueurs des abondances!

4

Sur la crête du cœur hésitant:
quel sourire qui de la bouche
s'empare de celui qui hésite!
Quelle lenteur inédite
dans ce sourire. Quel chant
supprimé, dans ce sourire. Autant
de sérieux, autant de limite
que d'affranchissement.
Autant de fuite que de retour.
Quel sourire! On le dirait provocant
n'était-il pas, dans sa double audace,
trop complet, trop absent
pour avoir quiconque en face.

they surely needed blunter hearts
to be ravished by their cries.

Give up this sweet haggling.

But inside you, at the very depths of you,
what a cemetery! So many Gods acquitted,
dismissed, forgotten, out of use,
so many prophets, so many wise men
abandoned by your mad desire!

You have unpeopled the vast heavens.
And the dryads, deprived of their chance,
have re-entered the trees and advance
only in sap, spilling tears and tears. . . .
Springs deny themselves, and flowers,
bruised by inattentive violences,
deformed by vague inventors
who excite them to the bitter end,
blossom without saying. . . . Everything's afraid
of you: poor killers of abundances!

4

On the crest of the hesitating heart:
what a smile seizes
the mouth of the hesitant!
What unprecedented slowness
in that smile. What suppressed
song in that smile. And as much
gravity, as much limit
as emancipation.
As much flight as return.
What a smile! We'd call it provocative
if, in its double audacity, it weren't
too complete, too absent
to face anyone.

Tombeaux

1

C'est donc à cela que ta vie fut un tendre prélude:
les inavoués, les absents se montrent ton cœur!
Au lieu de t'appeler au soleil à la fin des études,
on évite ton nom comme le nom d'une peur.

On évite ton nom que la pierre proclame sienne,
car l'événement qui aux pierres confère nos noms
pèse sur les voix des êtres qui se souviennent
cherchant de leur main égarée un aveu de leur front.

C'est donc à cela, à cette musique parfaite
que tout en toi consentait, amante et sœur.
La terre te chante; on sent l'élan de sa tête,
mais sa bouche est tournée ailleurs.

2

Encore, encore, je vais et je m'incline
devant la lente vie de ton tombeau;
à la pervenche et à l'aubépine
tu as cédé la paix de ton enclos.

Un jeune été a recouvert la dalle.
Tant de verdure vivant entre nous!
Et tu me tends la pâle digitale
où l'on n'accède que par en dessous.

Il faut que le frelon avide plonge
avant d'entrer dans l'antre transparent
des fleurs penchées; pour être de leur songe
on doit venir d'en bas ressurgissant.

Graves

1

It was to this, then, that your life was a tender prelude:
the unavowed, the absent show themselves your heart!
Instead of calling you to sunlight at the end of etudes,
we avoid your name like the name of some fear.

We avoid your name that stone proclaims its own,
for the event that confers our names on stone
weighs on the voices of those who recall
looking for their brow's consent with frantic hand.

It was to this, then, to this perfect music
that all in you consented, lover and sister.
The earth sings you; we feel the tilt of its head,
but its mouth is turned toward someplace else.

2

Again and again, I go and I lean
before the slow life of your grave;
you have surrendered your enclosure's peace
to the periwinkle and the hawthorn.

A young summer has recovered the marble.
So much living verdure between us!
And you offer me that pale digital
we cannot reach but from below.

The avid hornet has to dive
before it enters the transparent lair
of leaning flowers; to be their
dream, we must come rising from below.

Sommes-nous hauts, nous autres, les vivants,
et trop loin de la prochaine pose!
Le lit même nous soulève et l'on n'ose
te ressembler, Amie, en s'endormant. . . .

Les Trois Porteuses

LA PORTEUSE DE FLEURS

À Jean Cassou et à Ida Jankelevitch

Elles ne sont plus à moi, mes mains,
elles sont à ces fleurs que je viens de cueillir;
puissent-elles, ces fleurs, à l'imagination si pure,
inventer un autre être à ces mains
qui ne sont plus miennes. Alors,
obéissante, je me mettrai à côté de lui,
à côté de cet être, curieuse de mes mains anciennes
et je ne le quitterai plus, l'écoutant
de tout mon cœur, avant qu'il ne me dise:
Ô Légère!

LA PORTEUSE DE FRUITS

À Madame la mère de Jean Cassou

Voici ce que c'est que l'année.
Si ronds que vous soyez, vous n'êtes pas les têtes:
on vous a pensés là-bas, ô fruits achevés,
les hivers vous ont imaginés, calculés,
dans les racines et sous l'écorce des troncs
(à la lampe).
Mais sans doute êtes-vous plus beaux
que tous ces projets, ô vous, les œuvres aimées.
Et moi, je vous porte. Votre poids
me rend plus sérieuse que je ne suis.
J'exprime malgré moi je ne sais quel regret

We, the living, we others who still tower
too far from that future pose!
Even beds prop us up, and we don't dare
resemble you, Friend, as we fall asleep. . . .

The Three Carriers

THE FLOWER CARRIER

For Jean Cassou and for Ida Jankelevitch

My hands are no longer mine,
they belong to the flowers I've just plucked;
can these flowers, with such pure imagination,
invent another being for these hands
that are no longer mine? And then,
obedient, I'll stand at his side,
at that being's side, curious about my former hands,
and I will never leave him, listening
with all my heart, before he can say to me:
O light-fingered one!

THE FRUIT CARRIER

For Madame, mother of Jean Cassou

So this is what the year is.
Round as you are, you still are not heads:
you were thought of out there, O ripened fruit,
the winters imagined you, calculated you,
in the roots, under the bark of trunks
(in lamplight).
But still you are more beautiful
than all those plans, O you beloved works.
And I, I carry you. Your weight
makes me more serious than I am.
Despite myself, I betray some vague regret

semblable à celui de la fiancée étonnée
lorsqu'elle s'en va embrasser,
une à une, ses pâles amies d'enfance.

LA PORTEUSE DE L'EAU

À Madame et à Monsieur André Wurmser

Toi, qui semblais toute hâte à la fontaine,
depuis que je t'ai arrêtée dans ma cruche,
eau simple, quel calme t'occupe et que tu me pèses
de tes souvenirs. N'oublie rien! Car il faudra
que, rapidement, tu te racontes
sur la pente de notre soif, ô jeunesse liquide!
Ce n'est pas moi qui porterai atteinte
à ta nature en te serrant contre moi. Si tu savais
combien mes lèvres sont fraîches, même avant t'avoir bue,
et si mon cœur soudain me surmonte,
c'est comme le chant du rossignol:
demande-lui s'il connaît la sueur.

Deux Poèmes

1

Aime-moi, qu'il reste à ma bouche
un peu de ce sourire qui te plaît;
mon bras, trop enfantin, quand tu le touches,
demain, il s'éveillera parfait.

Je ne suis point de celles qui arrêtent
le doux passant, le pèlerin aimé;
il me suffit qu'à jamais je reflète
le Dieu pressé qui m'a comblée.

like that of the astonished bride
as she starts to embrace,
one by one, her pale childhood friends.

THE WATER CARRIER

For Madame and Monsieur André Wurmser

You, that in the fountain seemed all haste,
since I stopped you in my jug, simple water,
what calm possesses you and how your memories
weigh me down. Forget nothing! You will have
to tell your story rapidly
on the incline of our tongue, O liquid youth!
I am not the one who will injure
your nature as I hold you close to me. If you knew
how cool my lips are, even before drinking you,
and if my heart suddenly soars over me,
it's like the nightingale's song:
ask him if he ever sweats.

Two Poems

1

Love me, let a little of this smile
that pleases you linger on my mouth;
tomorrow, when you touch it,
my too-childish arm will awaken perfect.

I am not one of those who stops
the tender walker, the cherished pilgrim;
it is enough for me forever to reflect
the hurried God who has fulfilled me.

Mais qu'il se verse, que mon corps d'albâtre
soit le vase à le contenir—
ou bien qu'il me comtemple comme le pâtre
contemple l'astre qui devait surgir.

2

Qu'il me soit caché par votre main
ce lendemain trop proche que j'ignore;
ce sera un jour tout autre; son aurore
m'aveuglerait de son essor soudain.

Une fois seule, on sera bien forte
à l'ombre de ce sombre abandon,
mais si vous m'attirez vers sa maison,
faites de façon à me masquer la porte.

Gong

pour Suzanne B.

1

Bourdonnement épars, silence perverti,
tout ce qui fut autour, en mille bruits se change,
nous quitte et revient: rapprochement étrange
de la marée de l'infini.

Il faut fermer les yeux et renoncer à la bouche,
rester muet, aveugle, ébloui:
l'espace tout ébranlé, qui nous touche
ne veut de notre être que l'ouïe.

Que suffirait? L'oreille peu profonde
déborde vite—et ne penche-t-on
contre la sienne, pleine de tous les sons
la vaste conque de l'oreille du monde?

But should he overflow, let my alabaster
body be the vase to hold him—
or let him contemplate me as the shepherd
contemplates the star about to rise.

2

Let that too-near tomorrow I ignore
be hidden from me by your hand;
that will be a different day; its dawn
will blind me with its sudden soar.

Only once will we be very strong
in this dark abandon's shade,
but if you draw me toward its house,
do so as to camouflage the door.

Gong

for Suzanne B.

1

A scattered humming, perverted silence,
all that was around changes to a thousand noises,
leaves us and returns: the strange harmony
of infinity's tide.

We must close our eyes, renounce our mouths,
remain mute, blind, and dazzled:
with space utterly shaken, what touches us
wants no more from our being than attention.

Who will suffice? The shallow ear
quickly overflows—and, against our own,
do we not tilt, full of every sound,
the vast conch of the world's ear?

2

Comme si l'on était en train
de fondre des Dieux d'airain,
pour y ajouter encor
des Dieux massifs, tout en or,
qui en bourdonnant se défont.
Et de tous ces Dieux qui s'en vont
en de flambants métaux,
s'élèvent d'ultimes sons
royaux!

Das Kleine Weinjahr

1

Le souvenir de la neige
d'un jour à l'autre s'efface;
la terre blonde et beige
réapparaît à sa place.

Une bêche alerte
déjà (écoute!) opère;
on se rappelle que verte
est la couleur qu'on préfère.

Sur les coteaux on aligne
tantôt un tendre treillage;
donnez la main à la vigne
qui vous connaît et s'engage.

2

As if we were
melting down bronze Gods
to add to them more
massive Gods of gold
that shatter as they hum.
And from all those Gods
departing in the flaming metals
rise ultimate and royal
sounds!

Das Kleine Weinjahr

1

The memory of snow
is erased from day to day;
instead, the blonde
and beige earth reappears.

A spade, alert,
already (listen!) works;
you remember green
is the color you prefer.

Then on the hillsides you align
the tender trellises;
you give a hand to the vine
who knows you and agrees.

2

Comme aux Saintes-Maries, là-bas,
dans l'indescriptible tourmente,
celui qui d'un coup se vante
d'être guéri, s'en va,
jetant sa béquille ardente:
ainsi la vigne, absente
a jeté ses échalas.

Tant de béquilles qui gisent
grises sur la terre grise;
le miracle est donc accompli?
Où est-elle, la Vigne? Elle marche,
elle danse sans doute devant l'arche. . . .

Heureux ceux qui l'auront suivie!

Souvenirs de Muzot

(en février 1924)
À Alice Bailly

I

Nous vivons sur un ancien sol d'échange,
où tout se donne, tout se rend—
mais notre cœur souvent échange l'Ange
contre la vanité d'un ciel absent.

Le pain naïf, l'outil de tous les jours,
l'intimité des choses familières,
qui n'est capable de les laisser pour
un peu de vide où l'envie prospère.

Mais même ce vide, si nous le tenons
bien contre nous, s'échauffe et s'anime,

2

As at the Saintes-Maries out there,
in unutterable torment,
someone who suddenly boasting
he is cured, walks off,
discarding his ardent crutch:
so the absent vine
has thrown off her stakes.

So many crutches crumbling
gray on the gray ground;
is the miracle accomplished, then?
The Vine, where is she? She is walking,
no doubt she is dancing before the arch. . . .

How happy are those who followed her!

Memories of Muzot

(February 1924)
For Alice Bailly

I

We live on an ancient bartering ground
where all is given, all surrendered—
but our heart often swaps an Angel
for the vanity of an absent sky.

The naive bread, the common tool,
the intimacy of familiar things,
who can't leave them for a little
emptiness where longing grows.

But even that void, if we hold it
close to us, warms up and stirs,

et l'Ange, pour le rendre légitime,
l'entoure doucement d'un violon.

II / 1

De loin le printemps à venir
nous souffle un peu de sa chance;
notre longue patience
va-t-elle enfin aboutir

à ce que l'on aime reconnaître,
à ce flottant bonheur
qui nous portera . . . ou peut-être
en sera-t-on le porteur?

II / 2

Bientôt ce sera à la vigne
de se remettre au clair;
j'attends déjà qu'on aligne
les échalas comme des vers.

Quel adorable poème
l'on écrira sur les coteaux!
Et ce sera le soleil même
qui le jugera beau.

II / 3

Mais d'abord, rentrons au feu.
Ce vent trompeur, qu'il frôle
les arbres, et s'il console,
que ce soit pour eux.

and the Angel, just to make it legal,
surrounds it softly with a violin.

II / 1

From afar the coming spring
breathes some of its possibility
toward us; will our long
patience finally bloom

in what we love to recognize,
in a floating happiness
that will carry us . . . or, perhaps,
will we be its carrier?

II / 2

Soon it will be up to the vine
to restore itself in light;
I'm already waiting for the props
to be aligned like lines.

What an adorable poem will
be written on the hillsides!
And it will be the sun itself
that will rule it beautiful.

II / 3

But first, let's go back to the fire.
Let this deceptive wind breeze
the trees, and if it comforts,
let that be for them.

Rentrons à ceux qui écrivent,
et puis, saluons enfin
la tendre saison portative
qu'Alice Bailly peint!

Le Noyer

À Madame Jeanne de
Sépibus-de Preux

1

Arbre qui, de sa place,
fièrement arrondit
tout autour cet espace
de l'été accompli,

arbre dont le volume
rond et abondant
prouve et résume
ce que l'on attend longtemps:

j'ai pourtant vu rougir
tes feuilles en devenant vertes:
de cette pudeur offerte
ta magnificence, certes,
les veut à présent punir.

II

Arbre, toujours au milieu
de tout ce qui l'entoure—
arbre qui savoure
la voûte entière des cieux,

Let's go in to those who write,
and celebrate at last
the tender portable season
that Alice Bailly paints!

Walnut Tree

For Madame Jeanne de
Sépibus-de Preux

I

Tree that from its place
proudly rounds out
all around this space
of the completed summer,

tree whose very volume,
round and abundant,
proves and then resumes
what we attend so long:

and yet I saw your leaves
redden while becoming green:
with this proffered blush,
in fact, your magnificence
now wants to punish them.

II

Tree, ever at the center
of whatever it surrounds—
tree that savors
the entire vault of heaven,

toi, comme aucun autre,
tourné vers partout:
on dirait un apôtre
qui ne sait pas d'où

Dieu lui va apparaître....
Or, pour qu'il soit sûr,
il développe en rond son être
et lui tend des bras mûrs.

III

Arbre qui peut-être
pense au dedans:
antique Arbre-Maître
parmi les arbres servants!

Arbre qui se domine,
se donnant lentement
la forme qui élimine
les hasards du vent:

plein de forces austères
ton ombre claire nous rend
une feuille qui désaltère
et des fruits persévérants.

Muzot, écrit le 12 juin 1924

you, like nothing else,
turned in all directions:
as if you're an apostle
who doesn't know from whence

God will appear to him. . . .
So, in order to be sure,
he develops himself round,
and tends him tempered arms.

III

Tree that inside,
perhaps, can think:
ancient Master-Tree
among the servant trees!

Tree that rules itself
by assuming, slowly,
form that discards
the hazards of wind:

full of austere powers,
your dear shade offers
us a refreshing leaf
and persevering fruit.

Muzot, written June 12, 1924

Le Petit Cahier

À Mademoiselle Contat

1: ROSSIGNOL

Rossignol·... dont le cœur
plus que des autres exulte,
prêtre d'amour, dont le culte
est un culte d'ardeur.

Ô charmant troubadour
de la nuit qui te hante,
tu brodes l'échelle sonnante
sur son abîme de velours.

C'est toi la voix des sèves
qui dans les arbres se tait;
mais à nous, Rossignol, tes élèves,
tu imposes le même secret.

2: MÉSANGE

Ô toi, petit cœur, qui hivernes
avec nous au milieu des rigueurs,
tu te poses—tendre lanterne
de vie—sur les arbres en pleurs;

je contemple ce feu qui t'allume
à travers ton plumage dru,
et moi, plus caché à la brume
je ne crains de m'éteindre non plus.

A-t-elle peur de demain cette neige?
En effet, elle durcit en vain;
mais nous, qu'une flamme protège,
nous aurons la joie de demain.

Small Notebook

For Mademoiselle Contat

1: NIGHTINGALE

Nightingale . . . whose heart
exults more than others',
priest of love, whose cult
is the cult of ardor.

O charming troubadour
of the night obsessing you,
you embroider a resounding ladder
on its abyss of velvet.

You are the voice of saps
that in the trees keeps quiet;
but, Nightingale, to us, your students,
you keep assigning the same secret.

2: TITMOUSE

O you, small heart that winters
out these bitter winter days with us
—tender lantern of life—
you perch on the weeping trees;

I reflect on the fire shining
through your thickset feathers,
and I, more hidden by the mist,
I'm not afraid to burn out, either.

Does this snow fear tomorrow?
In fact, it hardens in vain;
but we, protected by a flame,
we'll know the pleasure of tomorrow.

Chanson orpheline

I

Où veux-tu que je m'en aille?
Partout m'attendent ces mots. . . .
Après tous les jours de travail,
après tous les nuits de repos,
après toutes les larmes et les rires
qui se sont écoulées,
après tout que je hais, que j'admire
dans cette chaîne de change
revient le refrain étrange,
qui me fait désespérer.

Est-ce toi mon père? Tu te vantes
que toutes les femmes charmantes
le long de ta vie t'aimaient trop.
Est-ce ma mère, qui chante
dans son pauvre tombeau?

II

Aucune de mes amies
ne m'a compris
quand je pleure dans l'église
elles me disent:
C'est la vie.

Aucun de mes jours
ne me prend par la main,
j'attends en vain,
que je crains:
l'amour.

Aucune de mes nuits
ne m'apporte quelque chose:

Orphan Song

I

Where do you want me to go?
Those words wait for me everywhere. . . .
After all the days of work,
after all the nights of rest,
after all the laughs and tears
that have slipped away,
after all I hate, all I admire
in this chain of change,
comes the strange refrain
that drives me to despair.

Is it you, my father? You boast
that all those charming women
in your life loved you too much.
Is this my mother, singing
in her wretched grave?

II

None of my friends
has understood me;
when I weep in church
they tell me:
That's life.

None of my days
holds my hand;
I wait in vain
for what I dread:
love.

None of my nights
brings me something:

une tendresse,
qui me presse,
un rêve, une rose....
Je n'ose
de croire que c'est la vie....

Mensonges I

1

Mensonge, arme d'adolescent,
arrachée à la forge du hasard
toute brûlante.... Poignard,
saisi n'importe comment.
Clôture bâclée, brusque mur!
Corps et geste sans tête
auxquels, éperdument, on prête
un visage trop pur.
Plante soudaine et hybride
qui, poussant dans le vide
atteint parfois trois mètres de haut,
et se fane trop tôt
pour n'avoir connu aucune saison.
Maison, belle maison,
trop belle pour nous qui vivons dehors,
maison qui a tort
parce qu'on ignore....
Maison trop durable encore
en face de la mort.

2

Toi, ô pauvre, que te cramponnes
et qui, de peur, frémis quand on sonne,
tu as des sœurs si grandes et si pures

a tenderness
that holds me close,
a dream, a rose.....
I don't dare
believe that's life.

Lies I

1

Lie, adolescent weapon,
torn from the fiery forge
of risk.... Dagger
grabbed any which way.
Makeshift fence, improvised wall!
Headless body and gesture
to which, frantically, we lend
a too-pure face.
Sudden, hybrid plant
which, growing in the void,
sometimes reaches three yards high
and withers far too soon
for having known no season.
House, handsome house,
too handsome for us who live outdoors,
house that's wrong
because we ignore....
House still too durable
when face-to-face with death.

2

Poor thing, clutching yourself,
trembling with fright when we ring,
your sisters are so grand and pure

que les siècles, à force d'en prendre mesure,
s'épuisent. Adolescent qui se ronge,

ami d'enfance, naïf mensonge,
sens-tu toujours, lorsqu'on te préfère,
dans la révolte qui te redresse,
ta famille pleine de déesses
et ces dieux hautains, tes beaux-frères?

3

Cimetière compromettant,
plein de résurrections évitables;
perroquets ivres de mots palpables
dont leur langue imperméable
s'éprend. . . .
Goût de fruits peints.
Parfum de calices
que de vagues institutrices
avaient brodés sur des coussins.

Mensonges II

1

Mensonge, jouet que l'on casse.
Jardin où l'on change de place,
pour mieux se cacher;
où pourtant, parfois, on jette un cri,
pour être trouvé à demi.

Vent, qui chante pour nous,
ombre de nous, qui s'allonge.
Collection de beaux trous
dans notre éponge.

that centuries exhaust themselves trying
to measure them. Anxious adolescent,

childhood friend, naive lie,
since you're preferred, in the revolt
that sets you straight do you always feel
your family full of goddesses,
your brothers-in-law, those haughty gods?

3

Compromising cemetery,
full of avoidable resurrections;
parrots drunk on palpable words,
their impervious tongue
infatuated with. . . .
Taste of painted fruit.
Perfume of calyxes
that some vague governess
embroidered on her cushions.

Lies II

1

Lie, plaything we shatter.
Garden where we change place
to hide ourselves better;
or, where we might let out a cry
just to be half-found.

Wind that sings for us,
our own shadow growing long.
Collection of the handsome
holes in our sponge.

2

Masque? Non. Tu es plus plein,
mensonge, tu as des yeux sonores.
Plutôt vase sans pied, amphore
qui veut qu'on la tient.

Tes anses, sans doute, ont mangé ton pied.
On dirait que celui qui te porte, t'achève,
n'était le mouvement dont il te soulève,
si singulier.

3

Es-tu fleur, es-tu oiseau,
mensonge? Es-tu à peine mot
ou mot et demi? Quel pur silence
t'entoure, bel îlot nouveau
dont les cartes ignorent la provenance.

Tard-venu de la création,
œuvre du huitième jour, posthume.
Puisque c'est nous qui te faisons,
il faut croire que Dieu te consume.

4

T'ai-je appelé? Mais de quel mot, de quel signe
suis-je coupable soudain,
si ton silence me crie, si ta paupière me cligne
d'un accord souterrain?

2

Mask? No. You're much fuller,
lie, you have resounding eyes.
Rather, a footless vase, amphora
that wants us to hold it up.

No doubt your handles ate your foot.
It seems what carries you, completes
you, is the very movement that lifts
you, so remarkable.

3

Are you flower, are you bird,
lie? Are you barely word
or word and a half? What pure
silence circles you, lovely new island
with origins that maps ignore.

Late-comer to creation,
posthumous work of the eighth day.
Since it's us who make you,
we must believe that God consumes you.

4

Did I call you? But of what word, of what sign
am I suddenly guilty,
if your silence cries to me, if your eyelid winks
at me with an underground agreement?

5

À ce sourire épars
comment trouver un visage?
On voudrait qu'une joue s'engage
à mettre ce fard.

Il y a du mensonge dans l'air,
comme, autrefois, cette marquise
qu'on a brûlée, toute grise
de la vie à l'envers.

6

Je ne m'explique point.
On ferme les yeux, on saute;
c'est chose presque dévote
avec Dieu en moins.

On ouvre les yeux après,
parce qu'un remord nous ronge:
à côté d'un si beau mensonge,
ne semble-t-on contrefait?

Mensonges III

1

On dit: j'ai rêvé, et non: j'ai menti.
On se réveille, on fait la refonte,
rentrant avec un peu de honte
dans la chambre anéantie.

L'ascenseur nous remet à l'étage,
dit «de la réalité» et s'en va.

5

How can we find a face
for that sparse smile?
We wish a cheek agreed
to wear that rouge.

There is lying in the air,
just as, before, the awning
that we burned, utterly gray
from living upside down.

6

I don't make myself clear.
We close our eyes, we leap;
with God at least
such an act's almost devout.

Later we open our eyes
because remorse is gnawing us:
next to such a handsome lie,
don't we seem counterfeit?

Lies III

1

We say: I dreamt, and not: I lied.
We awaken, we do some rearranging,
re-entering, somewhat ashamed,
into the devastated room.

The elevator returns us to our floor,
says, "a little truth," and leaves.

Et on montre aux choses sages
sa figure de mardi gras.

2

Y a-t-il davantage en fait de mensonge?
Cela dépend du chasseur et de la chasse.
Celui qui revient à la surface
est toujours un autre que celui qui plonge.

Quelques Œufs de Pâques

(pour 1926)

1

C'était un de ces premiers papillons
qui à peine trouvent des fleurs.
Corde avant le violon,
précoce précurseur.

Que le monde lui semblait grand
et surtout peu meublé;
d'appartement en appartement,
tout était à louer.

Mais les maçons n'avaient point fini,
et le vitrier sifflait tout haut.
Le beau monsieur s'en va indécis:
parmi ces ouvriers peu polis
mettre ses bibelots!

And to those wise things
we bare our mardi gras face.

   2

Is there more, in fact, to lies?
That depends on the hunter and the hunt.
The one returning to the surface
is always different from the one who dives.

A Few Easter Eggs

(for 1926)

   1

He was one of those first butterflies
that barely finds a flower.
String before the violin,
a precocious precursor.

How the world seemed large to him
and so sparsely furnished;
from apartment to apartment,
everything was up for rent.

But the masons hadn't finished
and the glass maker whistled loud.
The fine gentleman leaves unsettled:
to place one's bric-a-brac
among such unpolished laborers!

2

Toute fleur n'est qu'une mince fontaine
qui tantôt revient de son élan éperdu.
L'arbre aussi redescend en dedans de sa gaine,
comme s'il eût rencontré un refus.

Vous seul, pauvre Dieu, jadis, vous prîtes un tel
recul sur la route de la misère humaine,
qu'on dirait que la longue absence de votre bond dans le ciel
commence à peine.

3

Qui sait, si les Anges ne demandaient point:
Celui, quand la mort l'enserre,
rejettera-t-il son tombeau loin
comme un manteau de terre?

Dans la mort qui nous glace, il eut trop chaud:
Il y mûrit sa violence. . . .
Caressons lentement sur l'Agneau
la laine de son absence.

2

Each flower's only a thin fountain
returning quickly from its frantic leap.
The tree also drops back into its sheath,
as if it had encountered a rejection.

Poor God, only you, once, took such
a backward fall on the road of human misery,
that the long absence of your leap into heaven
seems barely just begun.

3

Who knows if the Angels didn't ask:
When death surrounds him,
will he throw off his grave
like a cloak of earth?

In the death that freezes us, he was too warm:
He ripened its violence. . . .
On the Lamb let us slowly stroke
the wool of his absence.

Tendres Impôts à la France

Affectionate Taxes to France

for

ARCHIBALD MACLEISH

on his 90th birthday

Tendres Impôts à la France

1: LE DORMEUR

Laissez-moi dormir, encore. . . . C'est la trêve
pendant de longs combats promise au dormeur;
je guette dans mon cœur la lune qui se lève,
bientôt il ne fera plus si sombre dans mon cœur.

Ô mort provisoire, douceur qui nous achève,
mesure de mes cimes, très juste profondeur,
limbes de tout mon sang, et innocence des sèves,
dans toi, à sa racine, ma peur même n'est pas peur.

Mon doux seigneur Sommeil, ne faites pas que je rêve
et mêlez en moi mes ris avec mes pleurs;
laissez-moi diffus, pour que l'interne Ève
ne sorte de mon flanc en son hostile ardeur.

2: PÉGASE

Cheval ardent et blanc, fier et clair Pégase,
après ta course—ah, que ton arrêt est beau!
Sous toi, cabré soudain, le sol que tu écrases
avale l'étincelle et donne de l'eau!

La source qui jaillit sous ton sabot dompteur,
à nous, qui l'attendons, est d'un secours suprême;
sens-tu que sa douceur impose à toi-même?
Car ton cou vigoureux apprend la courbe des fleurs.

Affectionate Taxes to France

1: THE SLEEPER

Please let me sleep again. . . . During long
battles it's the truce promised to the sleeper;
I watch the moon as it rises in my heart,
soon it won't be so dark at my center.

O provisionary death, sweetness that does us in,
measure of my heights, depth's fine precision,
the innocence of sap, all of my blood's limbs,
in you, at its root, even my fear isn't fear.

My sweet lord, Sleep, don't make me dream,
and mingle in me my laughs with my tears;
leave me diffused so the internal Eve
won't rise from my side in her hostile ardor.

2: PEGASUS

Ardent and white horse, bright, proud Pegasus,
after your run—ah, how your stop is beautiful!
Under you, suddenly reared, the ground you crush
swallows the spark and gives back water!

To us who've waited, the spring gushing under
your taming hoof is a supreme relief;
do you feel its sweetness mastering you?
For your tough neck learns the bow of flowers.

3

Qu'est-ce que les Rois Mages
ont-ils pu apporter?
Un petit oiseau dans sa cage,
une énorme Clef

de leur lointain royaume—
et le troisième du baume
que sa mère avait préparé
d'une étrange lavande

de chez eux.
Faut pas médire de si peu,
puisque ça a suffi à l'enfant
pour devenir Dieu.

4: À UNE AMIE

Combien cœur de Marie est exposé,
non seulement au soleil et à la rosée:
tous les sept glaives l'ont trouvé.
Combien cœur de Marie est exposé.

Ton cœur pourtant me semble plus à l'abri,
malgré le malheur qui en a tant envie,
il est moins exposé que le cœur de Marie.

Le corps de Marie ne fut point une chose;
ta poitrine sur ton cœur est beaucoup plus close,
et même si ta douleur veut qu'il s'expose:
il n'est jamais plus exposé qu'une rose.

3

What could those Three
Kings really bring?
A tiny bird in a cage,
an enormous key

from a distant empire—
and the third,
some native balm
of mysterious lavender

his mother had concocted.
We mustn't minimize so little,
since it sufficed the child
to become God.

4: TO A FRIEND

Mary's heart's so unprotected,
not only from the sun and dew:
all seven swords also found it.
Mary's heart's so unprotected.

Your heart seems to me more sheltered,
despite the grief that envies it,
it's less exposed than Mary's heart.

Mary's body wasn't made of flesh;
your heart lies close beneath your breast,
and even if your grief wants it exposed:
it's never unprotected like a rose.

5

Restons à la lampe et parlons peu;
tout ce qu'on peut dire ne vaut pas l'aveu
du silence vécu; c'est comme le creux
d'une main divine.
Elle est vide, certes, la main, cette main;
mais une main ne s'ouvre jamais en vain,
et c'est elle qui nous combine.

Ce n'est pas la nôtre: nous précipitons
les choses lentes. C'est déjà l'action
qu'une main qui se montre. Regardons
la vie qui en elle afflue.
Celui qui bouge n'est pas le plus fort.
Il faut admirer son tacite accord
avant que la force remue.

6: «L'INDIFFÉRENT» (Watteau)

Ô naître ardent et triste,
mais, à la vie convoqué,
être celui qui assiste,
tendre et bien habillé,

à la multiple surprise
qui ne vous engage point,
et, bien mis, à la bien mise
sourire de très loin.

5

Let's stay by the lamp and say little;
all we can say isn't worth the avowal
of silence lived; it's like the pit
of a divine hand.
The hand is empty, surely, this hand;
but a hand never opens in vain,
and we're combined by this one.

It isn't ours: we accelerate
slow things. An opening hand
is already action. Let's look
at the life that flows in it.
The one that moves isn't the strongest.
We must admire its tacit harmony,
before power starts to stir.

6: "L'INDIFFÉRENT" (Watteau)

Oh, to be born ardent and sad
but, summoned to this life,
to be the one who, tender and
well-dressed, is present

at the multiple surprise
in which he's not involved
and, well-off, smiles
at a well-off woman from afar.

7: PRIÈRE DE LA TROP PEU INDIFFÉRENTE

Aidez les coeurs, si soumis et si tendres—
tout cela blesse!
Qui saurait bien la tendresse défendre
de la tendresse.

Pourtant la lune, clémente déesse,
ne blesse aucune.
Ah, de nos pleurs où elle tombe sans cesse,
sauvez la lune!

8

Reste tranquille, si soudain
l'Ange à ta table se décide;
efface doucement les quelques rides
que fait la nappe sous ton pain.

Tu offriras ta rude nourriture
pour qu'il en goûte à son tour,
et qu'il soulève à sa lèvre pure
un simple verre de tous les jours.

Ingénuement, en ouvrier céleste,
il prête à tout une calme attention;
il mange bien en imitant ton geste,
pour bien bâtir à ta maison.

9

Il faut croire que tout est bien, si tant
de calme suit à tant d'inquiétude;
la vie, à nous, se passe en prélude,
mais parfois le chant qui nous surprend
nous appartient, comme à son instrument.

7: PRAYER OF ONE NOT INDIFFERENT ENOUGH

Help the hearts so submissive and soft—
all that wounds!
Who knows how to defend tenderness
against tenderness enough.

And yet the moon, that merciful goddess,
wounds no one.
Ah, from our tears where she always falls,
save the moon!

8

Stay still, if the Angel
at your table suddenly decides;
gently smoothe those few wrinkles
in the cloth beneath your bread.

Then offer him your own rough food
so he can have his turn to taste,
so he can raise to that pure lip
a simple, common glass.

Ingenious celestial carpenter,
he lends all a calm attention;
he eats well, imitating your gesture,
so he can build well on your house.

9

We must believe that all is well
if such calm follows such anxiety;
we live our life in prelude,
but sometimes a surprising song
belongs to us, as to its instrument.

Main inconnue.... Au moins est-elle heureuse,
lorsqu'elle parvient à rendre mélodieuses
nos cordes? —Ou l'a-t-on forcée
de mêler même aux sons de la berceuse
tous les adieux inavoués?

10

Ce soir mon cœur fait chanter
des anges qui se souviennent....
Une voix, presque mienne,
par trop de silence tentée,

monte et se décide
à ne plus revenir;
tendre et intrépide,
à quoi va-t-elle s'unir?

11

Lampe du soir, ma calme confidente,
mon cœur n'est point par toi dévoilé;
on s'y perdrait peut-être; mais sa pente
du côté sud est doucement éclairée.

C'est encore toi, ô lampe d'étudiant,
qui veut que le liseur de temps en temps
s'arrête étonné et se dérange
sur son bouquin, te regardant.

(Et ta simplicité supprime un Ange.)

Unknown hand. . . . At least is it happy
when it manages to make our strings
melodious?—Or was it forced
to mingle even with the cradle-song
all those unavowed goodbyes?

10

Tonight my heart makes
angels sing, remembering. . . .
Lured by too much silence,
some voice, barely mine,

rises and decides
never to return;
tender and intrepid,
what will it unite with?

11

Night light, my calm confidante,
my heart's not bared by you; (we might
lose each other); but the slope
of its South side is softly lit.

It's still you, O student lamp,
who wants the reader, now and then,
to stop and be distracted at his desk
as he stares at you, astounded.

(And your simplicity supplants an Angel.)

12

Parfois les amants ou ceux qui écrivent
trouvent des mots qui, bien qu'ils s'effacent,
laissent dans un cœur une place heureuse
à jamais pensive. . . .

Car il en naît sous tout ce qui passe
d'invisibles persévérances;
sans qu'ils creusent aucune trace
quelques-uns restent des pas de la danse.

13

L'aurai-je exprimé, avant de m'en aller,
ce cœur qui, tourmenté, consent à être?
Étonnement sans fin, qui fus mon maître,
jusqu'à la fin t'aurai-je imité?

Mais tout surpasse comme un jour d'été
le tendre geste qui trop tard admire;
dans nos paroles écloses, qui respire
le pur parfum d'identité?

Et cette belle qui s'en va, comment
la ferait-on passer par une image?
Son doux ruban flottant vit davantage
que cette ligne qui s'éprend.

12

Sometimes lovers or writers
find words that, though they erase,
in one heart leave a happy place
that's thoughtful forever. . . .

Because an invisible perseverance
is born beneath all that passes;
without stamping the slightest trace,
some of the dance-steps remain.

13

Will I have expressed it before I leave,
this heart that, tormented, consents to be?
Endless astonishment that mastered me,
will I have imitated you up to the end?

But, like a summer day, all else pales
the tender gesture that admires too late;
from our words in bloom, who inhales
the pure fragrance of identity?

And that departing woman,
how can she be made into metaphor?
Her soft ribbon flutters, livelier
than this infatuated line.

14: TOMBEAU

[dans un parc]

Dors au fond de l'allée,
tendre enfant, sous la dalle;
on fera le chant de l'été
autour de ton intervalle.

Si une blanche colombe
passait au vol là-haut,
je n'offrirais à ton tombeau
que son ombre qui tombe.

15

De quelle attente, de quel
regret sommes-nous les victimes,
nous qui cherchons des rimes
à l'unique universel?

Nous poursuivons notre tort
en obstinés que nous sommes;
mais entre les torts des hommes
c'est un tort tout en or.

14: GRAVE

[in a park]

At the end of the path,
sleep under stone, sweet child;
we'll sing a summer song
around your interval.

Should one white dove
soar high overhead,
I'd offer your grave
only its shedding shadow.

15

Of what anticipation,
what regret are we the victims,
we who search for rhymes
for this unmatched universal?

Obstinates that we are,
we pursue our mistakes;
but among men's mistakes
is that one golden error.

Les Quatrains Valaisans

The Valaisian Quatrains

for
ARCHIBALD MACLEISH
on his 90th birthday

Les Quatrains Valaisans

1: PETITE CASCADE

Nymphe, se revêtant toujours
de ce qui la dénude,
que ton corps s'exalte pour
l'onde ronde et rude.

Sans repos tu changes d'habit,
même de chevelure;
derrière tant de fuite, ta vie
reste présence pure.

2

Pays, arrêté à mi-chemin
entre la terre et les cieux,
aux voix d'eau et d'airain,
doux et dur, jeune et vieux,

comme une offrande levée
vers d'accueillantes mains:
beau pays achevé
chaud comme le pain!

3

Rose de lumière, un mur qui s'effrite—
mais, sur la pente de la colline,
cette fleur qui, haute, hésite
dans son geste de Proserpine.

Beaucoup d'ombre entre sans doute
dans la sève de cette vigne;
et ce trop de clarté qui trépigne
au-dessus d'elle, trompe la route.

The Valaisian Quatrains

1: SMALL FOUNTAIN

Nymph, forever dressing
with what undresses you,
let your body be excited
for the round rough water.

You change your clothes,
even your hair, without rest;
behind such flight, your life
remains pure presence.

2

Landscape stopped halfway
between the earth and sky,
with voices of bronze and water,
ancient and new, tough and tender,

like an offering lifted
toward accepting hands:
lovely completed land,
warm, like bread!

3

Rose of light, a crumbling wall—
but, high on the incline
of the hill, that flower hesitates
as if she were Persephone.

No doubt a lot of shade is seeping
into this vine's sap;
and this excess light trampling
above her takes the wrong route.

4

Contrée ancienne, aux tours qui insistent
tant que les carillons se souviennent—
aux regards qui, sans être tristes,
tristement montrent leurs ombres anciennes.

Vignes où tant de forces s'épuisent
lorsqu'un soleil terrible les dore. . . .
Et, au loin, ces espaces qui luisent
comme des avenirs qu'on ignore.

5

Douce courbe le long du lierre,
chemin distrait qu'arrêtent des chèvres;
belle lumière qu'un orfèvre
voudrait entourer d'une pierre.

Peuplier, à sa place juste,
qui oppose sa verticale
à la lente verdure robuste
qui s'étire et qui s'étale.

6

Pays silencieux dont les prophètes se taisent,
    pays qui prépare son vin;
où les collines sentent encore la Genèse
    et ne craignent pas la fin!

Pays, trop fier pour désirer ce qui transforme,
    qui, obéissant à l'été,
semble, autant que le noyer et que l'orme,
    heureux de se répéter.

4

Ancient country with towers insisting
so much that carillons remember—
with features that, without being
sad, sadly show their ancient shadows.

Vines in which so much power is drained
as a terrible sun turns them gold. . . .
And, in the distance, those spaces
glowing like the futures we ignore.

5

Gentle curve along the ivy,
listless road where goats stop;
lovely light that a goldsmith
would bezel in a stone.

Poplar, in its proper place,
with its vertical opposing
the stretching and the sprawling
of a slow robust green.

6

Silent country whose prophets keep quiet,
    landscape preparing its wine;
where the hills are still feeling Genesis
    and do not fear the end!

Country, too proud to yearn for what transforms
    and which, obeying summer,
seems, as much as the walnut and the elm,
    happy to repeat itself.

Pays dont les eaux sont presque les seules nouvelles,
    toutes ces eaux qui se donnent,
mettant partout la clarté de leurs voyelles
    entre tes dures consonnes!

    7

Vois-tu, là-haut, ces alpages des anges
    entre les sombres sapins?
Presque célestes, à la lumière étrange,
    ils semblent plus que loin.

Mais dans la claire vallée et jusqu'aux crêtes,
    quel trésor aérien!
Tout ce qui flotte dans l'air et qui s'y reflète
    entrera dans ton vin.

    8

Ô bonheur de l'été: le carillon tinte
    puisque dimanche est en vue;
et la chaleur qui travaille sent l'absinthe
    autour de la vigne crépue.

Même à la forte torpeur les ondes alertes
    courent le long du chemin.
Dans cette franche contrée, aux forces ouvertes,
    comme le dimanche est certain!

    9

C'est presque l'invisible qui luit
au-dessus de la pente ailée;
il reste un peu d'une claire nuit
à ce jour en argent mêlée.

Country where about the only news is water,
    all this water giving itself,
leaving the light of its vowels everywhere
    between your hard consonants!

7

Up there, do you see alpine pastures for angels
    among the dark pines?
In that strange light, almost celestial,
    they seem more than far.

But in the bright valley, clear up to the crests,
    what aerial treasure!
Everything that floats in the air and reflects
    will enter your wine.

8

O summer's happiness: the carillon chimes
    because Sunday is in sight;
and the working heat can smell absinthe
    around the crinkled vine.

All along the road the brisk waters
    rush, even in this heavy lethargy.
In this free country with its open powers,
    how certain is a Sunday!

9

The invisible almost shines
above the winged slope;
some of the clear night remains
in this day mingled with silver.

Vois, la lumière ne pèse point
sur ces obéissants contours;
et, là-bas, ces hameaux, d'être loin,
quelqu'un les console toujours.

10

Ô ces autels où l'on mettait des fruits
avec un beau rameau de térébinthe
ou de ce pâle olivier—et puis
la fleur qui meurt, écrasée par l'étreinte.

Entrant dans cette vigne, trouverait-on
l'autel naïf, caché par la verdure?
La Vierge même bénirait la mûre
offrande, égrainant son carillon.

11

Portons quand même à ce sanctuaire
tout ce qui nous nourrit: le pain, le sel,
ce beau raisin . . . et confondons la mère
avec l'immense règne maternel.

Cette chapelle, à travers les âges,
relie d'anciens dieux aux dieux futurs,
et l'ancien noyer, cet arbre-mage,
offre son ombre comme un temple pur.

See, the light doesn't press down
on those obedient contours;
and out there, those hamlets, someone
always comforts them for being so far.

10

Oh, those altars where fruit was placed
with a lovely palm of terebinth
or of this pale olive tree—and
a dying flower, crushed by an embrace.

Entering this vineyard, will we find
a primitive altar hidden by the green?
Even the Virgin, beading her carillon,
would bless that ripened offering.

11

Even so, let us bring all that feeds
us to this sanctuary: bread, salt,
this lovely grape . . . and amaze the mother
with the immense maternal kingdom.

Through the ages this chapel
binds ancient gods to future gods,
and this ancient oak, this magnus-tree,
offers its shade like a pure temple.

12: LE CLOCHER CHANTE

Mieux qu'une tour profane,
je me chauffe pour mûrir mon carillon.
Qu'il soit doux, qu'il soit bon
aux Valaisannes.

Chaque dimanche, ton par ton,
je leur jette ma manne;
qu'il soit bon, mon carillon,
aux Valaisannes.

Qu'il soit doux, qu'il soit bon;
samedi soir dans les channes
tombe en gouttes mon carillon
aux Valaisans des Valaisannes.

13

L'année tourne autour du pivot
de la constance paysanne;
la Vierge et Sainte-Anne
disent chacune leur mot.

D'autres paroles s'ajoutent
plus anciennes encore—
elles bénissent toutes,
et de la terre sort

cette verdure soumise
qui, par un long effort,
donne la grappe prise
entre nous et les morts.

12: BELLTOWER'S SONG

More than a common tower,
I warm myself to ripen my carillon.
Let it be sweet, let it be good
to the Valaisian women.

I share my manna with them
every Sunday, tone by tone;
let my carillon be good
to the Valaisian women.

Let it be good, let it be sweet;
in the hamlets on Saturday night,
let my carillon fall in drops on
the Valaisian women's Valaisian men.

13

The year turns on the pivot
of a peasant perseverance;
the Virgin and Saint Anne
each have a word to say.

Other words are adding
themselves, even more ancient—
all give their blessing,
and from the earth arises

this obedient green
which, with long, hard work,
yields the cluster linked
between us and the dead.

14

Un rose mauve dans les hautes herbes,
un gris soumis, la vigne alignée. . . .
Mais au-dessus des pentes, la superbe
d'un ciel qui reçoit, d'un ciel princier.

Ardent pays qui noblement s'étage
vers ce grand ciel qui noblement comprend
qu'un dur passé à tout jamais s'engage
à être vigoureux et vigilant.

15

Tout ici chante la vie de naguère,
non pas dans un sens qui détruit le demain;
on devine, vaillants, dans leur force première
le ciel et le vent, et la main et le pain.

Ce n'est point un hier qui partout se propage
arrêtant à jamais ces anciens contours:
c'est la terre contente de son image
et qui consent à son premier jour.

16

Quel calme nocturne, quel calme
nous pénètre du ciel.
On dirait qu'il refait dans la palme
de vos mains le dessin essentiel.

La petite cascade chante
pour cacher sa nymphe émue. . . .
On sent la présence absente
que l'espace a bue.

14

In the tall grass, a mauve rose,
a subdued gray, the vineyard in rows. . . .
But above the slopes, the glory
of a receptive sky, a princely sky.

Ardent country nobly rising in tiers
toward a great sky that nobly knows
a hard past forever forces us
to be vigilant and vigorous.

15

Here, all sings the life of yesterday,
but not in a way that destroys tomorrow;
in their hardy primal powers, we sense
the wind and sky, the hand and bread.

It's not a proliferating past,
forever curbing these ancient contours:
it is the earth content with her own image
and consenting to her first day.

16

Such evening calm, such calm
penetrates us from the sky.
It seems to remake the essential
design in your hand's palm.

The little fountain sings
to hide its excited nymph. . . .
We feel the absent presence
that space has been drinking.

17

Avant que vous comptiez dix
tout change: le vent ôte
cette clarté des hautes
tiges de maïs,

pour la jeter ailleurs;
elle vole, elle glisse
le long d'un précipice
vers une clarté-sœur

qui déjà, à son tour,
prise par ce jeu rude,
se déplace pour
d'autres altitudes.

Et comme caressée
la vaste surface reste
éblouie sous ces gestes
qui l'avaient peut-être formée.

18

Chemin qui tourne et joue
le long de la vigne penchée,
tel qu'un ruban que l'on noue
autour d'un chapeau d'été.

Vigne: chapeau sur la tête
qui invente le vin.
Vin: ardente comète
promise pour l'an prochain.

17

Before you can count ten,
all changes: wind takes
the brightness from high
stalks of maize

to throw it on all sides;
it flies, it slides
along a precipice
toward a sister brightness

which, already taken up
in this rough game,
in turn moves herself
toward other altitudes.

And, as if caressed,
dazzled by these games
that maybe gave it shape,
the vast surface rests.

18

Road that turns and plays
along the leaning vineyard,
like a ribbon that we wind
around a summer hat.

Vineyard: hat on the head
that invents the wine.
Wine: blazing comet
promised for next year.

19

Tant de noir sérieux
rend plus âgée la montagne;
c'est bien ce pays très vieux
qui compte Saint-Charlemagne

parmi ses saints paternels.
Mais par en haut lui viennent,
à la secrète sienne,
toutes les jeunesses du ciel.

20

La petite clématite se jette
en dehors de la haie embrouillée
avec ce liseron blanc qui guette
le moment de se refermer.

Cela forme le long du chemin
des bouquets où des baies rougissent.
Déjà? Est-ce que l'été est plein?
Il prend l'automne pour complice.

21

Après une journée de vent,
dans une paix infinie,
le soir se réconcilie
comme un docile amant.

Tout devient calme, clarté. . . .
Mais à l'horizon s'étage,
éclairé et doré,
un beau bas-relief de nuages.

19

So much solemn black
makes the mountain look older;
no wonder this old country numbers
Saint Charlemagne among

its paternal saints.
But all the youth the sky
can give comes from on high
down into its secret self.

20

The small clematis tumbles
from the hedge that's tangled
with the morning glory watching
for that time to close again.

All along the road they make
bouquets where berries redden.
Is summer over? Already?
It picks autumn as accomplice.

21

After a day of wind,
the night is at ease
in an infinite peace
like a docile lover.

All turns calm, clear. . . .
But on the horizon, tiered,
glowing and gold,
a lovely bas-relief of clouds.

22

Comme tel qui parle de sa mère
lui ressemble en parlant,
ce pays ardent se désaltère
en se souvenant infiniment.

Tant que les épaules des collines
rentrent sous le geste commençant
de ce pur espace qui les rend
à l'étonnement des origines.

23

Ici la terre est entourée
de ce qui convient à son rôle
d'astre; tendrement humiliée,
elle porte son auréole.

Lorsqu'un regard s'élance: quel vol
par ces distances pures;
il faut la voix du rossignol
pour en prendre mesure.

24

Voici encore de l'heure qui s'argente,
mêlé au doux soir, le pur métal,
et qui ajoute à la beauté lente
les lents retours d'un calme musical.

L'ancienne terre se reprend et change:
un astre pur survit à nos travaux.
Les bruits épars, quittant le jour, se rangent
et rentrent tous dans la voix des eaux.

22

As someone speaking of his mother
will look like her while talking,
this ardent country slakes itself
by forever remembering.

So the shoulders of the hills
shrink beneath a gesture that begins
in this pure space that hauls them back
to the astonishment of origins.

23

Here the earth is surrounded
by whatever suits its role
as star; tenderly humiliated,
it bears its aureole.

When one look is launched: such flight
through these pure distances;
to take its measurements
you need the voice of nightingales.

24

Once again the hour's turning silver,
mingled with soft evening, the pure metal,
and it couples slow returns of musical
calm with a slower beauty.

The ancient earth recovers, changes:
a pure star survives our labor.
Leaving day, scattered noises re-arrange
themselves and re-enter the voice of waters.

25

Le long du chemin poussiéreux
le vert se rapproche du gris;
mais ce gris, quoique soumis,
contient de l'argent et du bleu.

Plus haut, sur un autre plan,
un saule montre le clair
revers de ses feuilles au vent
devant un noir presque vert.

À côté, un vert tout abstrait,
un pâle vert de vision,
entoure d'un fond d'abandon
la tour que le siècle défait.

26

Fier abandon de ces tours
qui pourtant se souviennent—
depuis quand jusqu'à toujours—
de leur vie aérienne.

Cet innombrable rapport
avec la clarté pénétrante
rend leur matière plus lente
et leur déclin plus fort.

27

Les tours, les chaumières, les murs,
même ce sol qu'on désigne
au bonheur de la vigne,
ont le caractère dur.

25

The whole length of the dusty road
the green is almost gray;
but this gray, although subdued,
is touched with silver and with blue.

Higher, on another plain,
a willow bares the bright back
 of its leaves to the wind
against a black that's almost green.

Nearby, an entirely abstract green,
the pale green of a vision,
with total unrestraint, surrounds
the tower that this century demolishes.

26

Proud crumbling of these towers
which, nonetheless, remember—
from who knows when to forever—
their towering life.

This constant contact
with the penetrating light
makes their matter slower
and their downfall harder.

27

Towers, walls, thatched huts,
even the earth we measure
off for the vineyard's sake,
have a tough character.

Mais la lumière qui prêche
douceur à cette austérité
fait une surface de pêche
à toutes ces choses comblées.

28

Pays qui chante en travaillant,
pays heureux qui travaille;
pendant que les eaux continuent leur chant,
la vigne fait maille pour maille.

Pays qui se tait, car le chant des eaux
n'est qu'un excès de silence,
de ce silence entre les mots
qui, en rythmes, avancent.

29

Vent qui prend ce pays comme l'artisan
qui, depuis toujours, connaît sa matière;
en la trouvant, toute chaude, il sait comment faire,
et il s'exalte en travaillant.

Nul n'arrêterait son élan magnifique; nul
ne saurait s'opposer à cette fougueuse audace—
et c'est encor lui qui, prenant un énorme recul,
tend à son œuvre le clair miroir de l'espace.

30

Au lieu de s'évader,
ce pays consent à lui-même;
ainsi il est doux et extrême,
menacé et sauvé.

But the light that preaches
tenderness to this austerity
creates a surface like a peach
on all the things it reaps.

28

Country singing while working,
happy working country;
while waters continue their song,
the vine grows link by link.

Country that keeps quiet because
the water's song is only an excess
of silence, of this silence between
words that advance in rhythm.

29

Wind that grips this country like a craftsman
who, from the start, has known his material;
finding it hot, he knows what must be done
and grows enthusiastic with his work.

No one could stop this magnificent momentum;
no one could oppose this fiery defiance—
and he is still the one who takes a long step back
to offer his work the bright mirror of space.

30

Rather than evade itself,
this country accepts itself;
so it's excessive and soft,
menaced and saved.

Il s'adonne avec ferveur
à ce ciel qui l'inspire;
il excite son vent et attire
par lui la plus neuve primeur

de cette inédite
lumière d'outre-mont:
l'horizon qui hésite
lui arrive par bonds.

31

Chemins qui ne mènent nulle part
entre deux prés,
que l'on dirait avec art
de leur but détournés,

chemins qui souvent n'ont
devant eux rien d'autre en face
que le pur espace
et la saison.

32

Quelle déesse, quel dieu
s'est rendu à l'espace,
pour que nous sentions mieux
la clarté de sa face.

Son être dissous
remplit cette pure
vallée du remous
de sa vaste nature.

Il aime, il dort.
Forts du Sésame,

It gets along fervently
with the inspiring sky;
it excites the wind and thus
attracts the newest freshness

of that primal light
from beyond the mountains:
the hesitating horizon
rushes toward it.

31

Roads leading nowhere
between two meadows,
as if detoured from their
end by design,

roads that often have
nothing ahead to face
but the season
and pure space.

32

What goddess, what god
came back to this place
so we could better feel
the brightness of its face.

Its atomized being
fills this pure
valley with the stirring
of its vast nature.

It loves. It sleeps.
We enter its body,

nous entrons dans son corps
et dormons dans son âme.

33

Ce ciel qu'avaient contemplé
ceux qui le loueront
pendant l'éternité:
bergers et vignerons,

serait-il par leurs yeux
devenu permanent,
ce beau ciel et son vent,
son vent bleu?

Et son calme après,
si profond et si fort,
comme un dieu satisfait
qui s'endort.

34

Mais non seulement le regard
de ceux qui travaillent les champs,
celui des chèvres prend part
à parfaire le lent

aspect de la Noble Contrée.
On la contemple toujours
comme pour y rester ou pour
l'éterniser

dans un si grand souvenir
qu'aucun ange n'osera,
pour augmenter son éclat,
intervenir.

the Caves of Sesame,
and, in its soul, sleep.

33

This sky contemplated
by those who will praise
it throughout eternity:
vine-growers, shepherds,

this beautiful sky,
its wind, its blue wind,
will it be made even more
permanent by their eyes?

And after, its calm,
so strong, so deep,
like a satisfied god
falling asleep.

34

Not only the gaze of those
who work the fields,
but also that of goats takes
part in perfecting the slow

aspect of this noble country.
We always contemplate it
as if to remain there, or maybe
to eternalize it

in so great a memory
that no angel, to brighten
its lustre, would dare
intervene.

35

Au ciel, plein d'attention,
ici la terre raconte;
son souvenir la surmonte
dans ces nobles monts.

Parfois elle paraît attendrie
qu'on l'écoute si bien—
alors elle montre sa vie
et ne dit plus rien.

36

Beau papillon près du sol,
à l'attentive nature
montrant les enluminures
de son livre de vol.

Un autre se ferme au bord
de la fleur qu'on respire:
ce n'est pas le moment de lire.
Et tant d'autres encore,

de menus bleus, s'éparpillent,
flottants et voletants,
comme de bleues brindilles
d'une lettre d'amour au vent,

d'une lettre déchirée
qu'on était en train de faire
pendant que la destinataire
hésitait à l'entrée.

35

Here the earth tells her story
to an attentive sky;
among these noble mountains
she is mastered by her memory.

Sometimes she seems touched
that we listen so well—
so she reveals her life
and then says nothing more.

36

A beautiful butterfly near
the earth is displaying
the illuminations of its flying
book to an attentive nature.

Another closes on the border
of the flower that we breathe:
this is not the time to read.
And still so many others,

fragile blues scattered,
floating and fluttering,
like the blue fragmenting
of a love letter in the wind,

of a torn-up letter
we had just been writing
while its addressee
hesitated at the door.

37: CIEL VALAISAN

Comment notre cœur lorsqu'il vibre
a-t-il tant besoin
que tout un ciel de loin
lui donne des conseils d'équilibre.

Mais ce ciel depuis toujours
a de nos cris l'habitude;
ami de la terre rude,
il en adoucit le contour.

38

Les hannetons ont fini leur ravage.
À ces rameaux déchus octroyés,
ils semblent pleins et innocents et sages,
comme s'ils étaient les fils du noyer.

Et l'arbre même ne se plaint qu'à peine,
car dans son vide guérit tant de bleu.
La vie s'attaque à la vie sans haine.
Elle abonde dans les prés heureux

où les grillons s'exaltent cri par cri.
Tout au milieu des jeunes vignes bouge
la tête d'une fille au foulard rouge
comme un point offert à tous ces i.

37: VALAISIAN SKY

Even as it thrills,
how our heart depends
on a whole distant sky
to offer stable counsel.

But this sky has always been
accustomed to our cries;
the friend of this rough earth
whose contours it tempers.

38

The locusts have finished their ravage.
To the sacrificed and dessicated boughs,
they seem full and innocent and sage,
as if they were the walnut's sons.

And even the tree barely complains,
for so much blue heals in its spaces.
Life is attacking life without hatred.
It abounds in the happy meadows

where crickets are impassioned, cry by cry.
At the very center of the young vines
the red-scarfed head of a girl moves
like a dot offered to each i.

Simple clocher trapu, au geste du semeur
qui jette aux sillons qu'avaient tracés les peines,
sans les compter jamais, les innombrables graines
d'anciennes sonneries, ces carillons du cœur.

La fleur qui les mûrit dans son calice pieux,
le beau fruit qui enfin les versa dans les cloches,
sombres bahuts d'airain, mis dans ce grenier proche
du ciel ... c'était la vie, la vie de tant d'aïeux.

La lente vie de ceux qui, lassés, laissent faire
du fond de leurs tombeaux, ou de ces autres dont
les crânes entassés au flanc des ossuaires
n'osent plus dire: nous dormons. ...

Les vieux, les petits ... ceux dont le départ précoce
avait brisé un clair et jeune consentement,
eux tous on fait la fleur et rempli cette crosse
d'où est tombé le trop d'un été abondant.

Le plus fort, le plus doux de leur essence pieuse
tombe autour de nous; taisons-nous, écoutons!
Le rythme du labeur, la joie vendangeuse,
de tous les espoirs la vie volumineuse
est entrée dans ces sons et survit en ces sons!

Peut-être, ce retour nous cherche-t-il à peine,
doucement nous frôlant s'adresse-t-il à Dieu,
à ces maisons, ces champs, à cette terre pleine
de tant de volonté et cachant tant de feu.

Mais, pourtant, dans nos cœurs, de leur côté champêtre,
recevons ce semis, dociles malgré nous,
et portons humblement, pour plaire aux ancêtres,
ce laborieux adieu qui les fit durs et doux.

Simple stocky belfry that with a sower's gesture,
and without ever counting them, scatters among furrows
traced with great pains the numberless grains
of ancient ringing bells, these carillons of the heart.

The flower that ripened them in its devoted calyx,
the lovely fruit that finally poured them into bells,
dark brass chests stored in this attic
near the sky, was . . . life, the life of so many yesterdays.

The slow life of those who, exhausted, from the depths
of their graves no longer care, or of those
whose skulls, stacked on the sides of charnel houses,
no longer dare to say: we sleep. . . .

The old, the small . . . those for whom a premature
departure broke a bright and young consent,
all those made the flower and refilled this staff
from which fell the excess of an abundant summer.

The strongest, the sweetest of their sacred essence
falls around us; let us be quiet and listen!
The rhythm of labor, the joy of harvest-time,
the voluminous life of all our dreams
has entered its sounds and survives in its sounds!

Perhaps this return hardly searches for us;
brushing us softly, it addresses itself to God,
to these houses, these fields, to this earth full
of so much will, and hiding so much fire.

And yet, docile despite ourselves, let us receive
this sowing in our hearts, in their rustic side,
and, to please our ancestors, let us humbly bear
this arduous adieu that made them tough and gentle.

Vergers

Orchards

Vergers

1

Ce soir mon cœur fait chanter
des anges qui se souviennent.…
Une voix, presque mienne,
par trop de silence tentée,

monte et se décide
à ne plus revenir;
tendre et intrépide,
à quoi va-t-elle s'unir?

2

Lampe du soir, ma calme confidente,
mon cœur n'est point par toi dévoilé;
(on s'y perdrait peut-être); mais sa pente
du côté sud est doucement éclairée.

C'est encore toi, ô lampe d'étudiant,
qui veux que le liseur de temps en temps
s'arrête, étonné, et se dérange
sur son bouquin, te regardant.

(Et ta simplicité supprime un Ange.)

3

Reste tranquille, si soudain
l'Ange à ta table se décide;
efface doucement les quelques rides
que fait la nappe sous ton pain.

Orchards

1

Tonight my heart makes
angels sing, remembering. . . .
Lured by too much silence,
some voice, barely mine,

rises and decides
never to return;
tender and intrepid,
what will it unite with?

2

Night light, my calm confidante,
my heart's not unveiled by you;
(we might lose ourselves); but the slope
of its South side is softly lit.

It's still you, O student lamp,
who wants the reader, now and then,
to stop and be distracted at his desk
as he stares at you, astounded.

(And your simplicity supplants an Angel.)

3

Stay still, if the Angel
suddenly chooses your table;
gently smooth those few wrinkles
in the cloth beneath your bread.

Tu offriras ta rude nourriture,
pour qu'il en goûte à son tour,
et qu'il soulève à la lèvre pure
un simple verre de tous les jours.

4

Combien a-t-on fait aux fleurs
d'étranges confidences,
pour que cette fine balance
nous dise le poids de l'ardeur.

Les astres sont tous confus
qu'à nos chagrins on les mêle.
Et du plus fort au plus frêle
nul ne supporte plus

notre humeur variable,
nos révoltes, nos cris—
sauf l'infatigable table
et le lit (table évanouie).

5

Tout se passe à peu près comme
si l'on reprochait à la pomme
d'être bonne à manger.
Mais il reste d'autres dangers:

celui de la laisser sur l'arbre,
celui de la sculpter en marbre,
et le dernier, le pire:
de lui en vouloir d'être en cire.

Then offer him your own rough food
so he can have his turn to taste,
so he can raise to that pure lip
a simple, common glass.

4

How many strange secrets
have we told the flowers
so that delicate balance
can tell us passion's weight.

All stars are confounded
when mingled with our grief.
From the frailest to the strong,
not one can still support

our ever-changing moods,
our revolts, our cries—
except the tireless table
and the bed (unconscious table).

5

Everything happens a little
as if we reproached the apple
for being good to eat.
But there are other risks:

to leave it on the tree,
to sculpt it out of marble,
and the last, the worst:
to wish that it were wax.

6

Nul ne sait, combien ce qu'il refuse,
l'Invisible, nous domine, quand
notre vie à l'invisible ruse
cède, invisiblement.

Lentement, au gré des attirances,
notre centre se déplace pour
que le cœur s'y rende à son tour:
lui, enfin Grand-Maître des absences.

7: PAUME

À Mme. et M. Albert Vulliez

Paume, doux lit froissé
où des étoiles dormantes
avaient laissé des plis
en se levant vers le ciel.

Est-ce que ce lit était tel
qu'elles se trouvent reposées,
claires et incandescentes,
parmi les astres amis
en leur élan éternel?

Ô les deux lits de mes mains,
abandonnés et froids,
légers d'un absent poids
de ces astres d'airain.

6

No one knows how mastered we are
by what the Invisible refuses
when, to the invisible ruse,
our life concedes, invisibly.

Slowly, at the will of fascinations,
our center starts to shift
so, in turn, the heart can yield:
it, at last, Grand-Master of absences.

7: PALM

For Mme. and M. Albert Vulliez

Palm, soft unmade bed,
where sleeping stars left
wrinkles as they rose
up toward the sky.

Was this bed such
that they are rested,
clear and incandescent,
among the friendly stars
in their eternal swirl?

Oh, the two beds of my hands,
abandoned and cold,
light with the absent load
of those brazen stars.

8

Notre avant-dernier mot
serait un mot de misère,
mais devant la conscience-mère
le tout dernier sera beau.

Car il faudra qu'on résume
tous les efforts d'un désir
qu'aucun goût d'amertume
ne saurait contenir.

9

Si l'on chante un dieu,
ce dieu vous rend son silence.
Nul de nous ne s'avance
que vers un dieu silencieux.

Cet imperceptible échange
qui nous fait frémir,
devient l'héritage d'un ange
sans nous appartenir.

10

C'est le Centaure qui a raison,
qui traverse par bonds les saisons
d'un monde à peine commencé
qu'il a de sa force comblé.

Ce n'est que l'Hermaphrodite
qui est complet dans son gîte.
Nous cherchons en tous les lieux
la moitié perdue de ces Demi-Dieux.

8

Our next-to-last word will be one
that is full of misery,
but, facing mother-conscience,
the very last one will be lovely.

Because we'll have to summon
every ounce of some desire
that no taste of bitterness
will know how to hinder.

9

If we sing a god, that god
offers us his silence.
None of us advances
but toward a silent god.

This imperceptible exchange
that makes us shiver
becomes an angel's heritage
we can never own.

10

The Centaur has good reason:
it leaps across the seasons
of a barely started world
that with its power it fulfilled.

Only the Hermaphrodite
is complete in its plight.
We search against the odds
for the lost half of these Half-Gods.

11: CORNE D'ABONDANCE

Ô belle corne, d'où
penchée vers notre attente?
Qui n'êtes qu'une pente
en calice, déversez-vous!

Des fleurs, des fleurs, des fleurs,
qui, en tombant, font un lit
aux bondissantes rondeurs
de tant de fruits accomplis!

Et tout cela sans fin
nous attaque et s'élance,
pour punir l'insuffisance
de notre cœur déjà plein.

Ô corne trop vaste, quel
miracle par vous se donne!
Ô cor de chasse, qui sonne
des choses, au souffle du ciel!

12

Comme un verre de Venise
sait en naissant ce gris
et la clarté indécise
dont il sera épris,

ainsi tes tendres mains
avaient rêvé d'avance
d'être la lente balance
de nos moments trop pleins.

11: CORNUCOPIA

O lovely horn, from where are you
curved toward our waiting?
No more than the leaning
of a calyx, pour yourself out!

Flowers, flowers, flowers,
that while falling make a bed
for the springing fullness
of so many finished fruits!

And all that endlessly
leaps out and attacks us
to punish the deficiency
of our heart already full.

O too-huge horn, what miracle
gives itself through you!
O hunting horn that rings
all things with heaven's breath!

12

As Venetian glass,
becoming, knows this gray
and cloudy brightness
will be its enchantment,

so your tender hands
had dreamed in advance
of being the slow balance
of our overflowing moments.

13: FRAGMENT D'IVOIRE

Doux pâtre qui survit
tendrement à son rôle
avec sur son épaule
un débris de brebis.
Doux pâtre qui survit
en ivoire jaunâtre
à son jeu de pâtre.
Ton troupeau aboli
autant que toi dure
dans la lente mélancolie
de ton assistante figure
qui résume dans l'infini
la trêve d'actives pâtures.

14: LA PASSANTE D'ÉTÉ

Vois-tu venir sur le chemin la lente, l'heureuse,
celle que l'on envie, la promeneuse?
Au tournant de la route il faudrait qu'elle soit
saluée par de beaux messieurs d'autrefois.

Sous son ombrelle, avec une grâce passive,
elle exploite la tendre alternative:
s'effaçant un instant à la trop brusque lumière,
elle ramene l'ombre dont elle s'éclaire.

15

Sur le soupir de l'amie
toute la nuit se soulève,
une caresse brève
parcourt le ciel ébloui.

13: IVORY FRAGMENT

Sweet shepherd tenderly
surviving in your role
with a sheep's shards
across your shoulder.
Sweet shepherd surviving
your shepherd's role
in a yellow ivory.
Your flock is lost
as much as you last
in the slow melancholy
of your staring face
that resumes in infinity
the living pasture's truce.

14: SUMMER PASSERBY

Do you see that slowly walking, happy
girl coming down the road, the one we envy?
At some turn in the road she ought to be
greeted by handsome men of days gone by.

Under her parasol, with passive grace,
she exploits the tender alternative:
disappearing briefly in the blinding light,
she gathers the shade of her incandescence.

15

The whole night rests
upon a lover's sigh,
a brief caress
crosses the dazzled sky.

C'est comme si dans l'univers
une force élémentaire
redevenait la mère
de tout amour qui se perd.

16

Petit Ange en porcelaine,
s'il arrive que l'on te toise,
nous t'avions quand l'année fut pleine
coiffé d'une framboise.

Ça nous semblait tellement futil
de te mettre ce bonnet rouge,
mais depuis lors tout bouge
sauf ton tendre tortil.

Il est desséché, mais il tient,
on dirait parfois qu'il embaume;
couronné d'un fantôme,
ton petit front se souvient.

17

Qui vient finir le temple de l'Amour?
Chacun en emporte une colonne;
et à la fin tout le monde s'étonne
que le dieu à son tour

de sa flèche brise l'enceinte.
(Tel nous le connaissons.)
Et sur ce mur d'abandon
pousse la plainte.

As if in the universe
an elemental power
again became the mother
of all love being lost.

16

Little porcelain Angel,
if they should take stock of you,
when the season reached its peak
we crowned you with a raspberry.

Capping you with that
red bonnet seemed so futile,
but since then all else trembles
except your tender coronet.

It is withered, but endures,
sometimes seeming to embalm;
crowned with such a phantom,
your little brow remembers.

17

Who's coming to finish Love's temple?
Each person brings a column;
and when it's done everyone is stunned
that the god, when his turn comes,

shatters the wall with his lance.
(That's how he is known.)
And on this wall of abandon
the complaint begins to grow.

18

Eau qui se presse, qui court—eau oublieuse
que la distraite terre boit,
hésite un petit instant dans ma main creuse,
souviens-toi!

Clair et rapide amour, indifférence,
presque absence qui court,
entre ton trop d'arrivée et ton trop de partance
tremble un peu de séjour.

19: EROS

I

Ô toi, centre du jeu
où l'on perd quand on gagne;
célèbre comme Charlemagne,
roi, empereur et Dieu—

tu es aussi le mendiant
en pitoyable posture,
et c'est ta multiple figure
qui te rend puissant.

Tout ceci serait pour le mieux;
mais tu es, *en nous* (c'est pire),
comme le noir milieu
d'un châle brodé de cachemire.

II

Ô faisons tout pour cacher son visage
d'un mouvement hagard et hasardeux.
Il faut le reculer au fond des âges
pour adoucir son indomptable feu.

18

Hurried, running water—forgetful water
drunk by a distracted land,
linger a while in my cupped hand,
               remember!

Between all that coming, all that leaving,
clear and rapid love, indifference,
almost a running absence,
               linger, trembling.

19: EROS

I

O you, center of the game
where we lose when we win;
famous as Charlemagne,
king, emperor and God—

you're also the mendicant
in a pitiful position,
and it's your shifting countenance
that makes you so powerful.

All this could be for the better;
but (it's worse) *in us,*
you're like the black center
of an embroidered cashmere shawl.

II

Oh, let's do all we can to hide his face
with a haggard and hazardous gesture.
We have to push him back into the abyss
of time to soften his untameable fire.

Il vient si près de nous qu'il nous sépare
de l'être bien-aimé dont il se sert;
il veut qu'on touche; c'est un dieu barbare
que des panthères frôlent au désert.

Entrant en nous avec son grand cortège,
il y veut tout illuminé—
lui, qui après se sauve comme d'un piège,
sans qu'aux appâts il ait touché.

III

Là, sous la treille, parmi le feuillage
il nous arrive de le deviner:
son front rustique d'enfant sauvage,
et son antique bouche mutilée....

La grappe devant lui devient pesante
et semble fatiguée de sa lourdeur;
un court moment on frôle l'épouvante
de cet heureux été trompeur.

Et son sourire cru, comme il l'infuse
à tous les fruits de son fier décor;
partout autour il reconnaît sa ruse
qui doucement le berce et l'endort.

IV

Ce n'est pas la justice qui tient la balance précise;
c'est toi, ô Dieu à l'envie indivise,
qui pèses nos torts,
et qui de deux cœurs qu'il meurtrit et triture
fais un immense cœur plus grand que nature,
qui voudrait encore

grandir.... Toi, qui indifférent et superbe,
humilies la bouche et exaltes le verbe
vers un ciel ignorant....

He comes so close to us, he separates
us from lovers he takes for his own use;
he wants us to touch; a barbarous god
that panthers brush by in deserts.

Entering us with his grand court,
he wants everything well-lit—
he, who then escapes as from a trap,
without having touched the bait.

III

Under the arbor, there, among the leaves
we happen to discover him:
the rustic forehead of his savage youth,
his ancient mutilated mouth. . . .

In front of him the grape gets heavier
and seems exhausted by its weight:
for one quick moment we brush by
this content, deceptive summer's terror.

And his raw smile—he can infuse
it into all the fruit of his vain scene;
all over he can recognize the ruse
that softly rocks him off to sleep.

IV

Justice doesn't hold the accurate scale;
it's you, O God of undivided envy,
who weighs our faults,
and from two murdered and ground hearts
makes one huge heart, bigger than nature,
that would still want

to grow. . . . You, haughty and indifferent,
who humiliates the mouth and exalts the word
toward an ignorant heaven. . . .

Toi qui mutiles les êtres en les ajoutant
à l'ultime absence dont ils sont des fragments.

20

Que le dieu se contente de nous,
de notre instant insigne,
avant qu'une vague maligne
nous renverse et pousse à bout.

Un moment nous étions d'accord:
lui, qui survit et persiste,
et nous dont le cœur triste
s'étonne de son effort.

21

Dans la multiple rencontre
faisons à tout sa part,
afin que l'ordre se montre
parmi les propos du hasard.

Tout autour veut qu'on l'écoute—
écoutons jusqu'au bout;
car le verger et la route
c'est toujours nous!

22

Les Anges, sont-ils devenus discrets!
Le mien à peine m'interroge.
Que je lui rende au moins le reflet
d'un émail de Limoges.

Et que mes rouges, mes verts, mes bleus
son œil rond réjouissent.

You, who mutilates beings while adding them
to the ultimate absence they're fragments of.

20

Let the god content himself with us,
with our notable instant,
before some vicious wave
overthrows and shatters us.

Once we were in accord:
him, who survives, persists,
and us, whose sad heart is
astounded by its very effort.

21

In the multiple encounter
let's offer everything its due,
so that order will appear
amidst hazard's propositions.

All things want us to listen—
let's listen to the very end;
because the orchard and the road
are always us!

22

Have the angels turned discreet!
Mine hardly questions me.
Let me offer him at least
the glow of Limoges glaze.

And let my reds, my greens, my blues
make his round eye rejoice.

S'il les trouve terrestres, tant mieux!
—pour un ciel en prémisses.

23

Combien le pape au fond de son faste,
sans être moins vénérable,
par la sainte loi du contraste
doit attirer le diable.

Peut-être qu'on compte trop peu
avec ce mouvant équilibre;
il y a des courants dans le Tibre:
tout jeu veut son contre-jeu.

Je me rappelle Rodin
qui me dit un jour d'un air mâle
(nous prenions, à Chartres, le train)
que, trop pure, la cathédrale
provoque un vent de dédain.

24

C'est qu'il nous faut consentir
à toutes les forces extrêmes;
l'audace est notre problème
malgré le grand repentir.

Et puis, il arrive souvent
que ce qu'on affronte, change:
le calme devient ouragan,
l'abîme le moule d'un ange.

Ne craignons pas le détour.
Il faut que les Orgues grondent,
pour que la musique abonde
de toutes les notes de l'amour.

If he finds them earthy, good!
—for a paradise of premises.

23

Without being less venerable
at the heart of his fast,
by the holy law of contrast
how the Pope must tempt the devil.

In this moving equilibrium
perhaps we put too little store;
there are crosscurrents in the Tiber:
each game needs its counter-game.

I recall Rodin
once saying in his cocky style
(we were leaving Chartres by train)
that, too pure, the cathedral
provokes a contemptuous wind.

24

It's that we must consent
to all extremes of power;
audacity's our problem,
despite the grand repentance.

And so, it often happens,
what we affront will change:
the calm turns into hurricane,
the abyss into an angel's mold.

We musn't dread that curve.
The Organs have to boom
for the music to abound
with all the notes of Love.

25

On a si bien oublié
les dieux opposés et leurs rites,
qu'on envie aux âmes confites
leur naïf procédé.

Il ne s'agit pas de plaire,
ni de se convertir,
pourvu que l'on sache obéir
aux ordres complémentaires.

26: LA FONTAINE

Je ne veux qu'une seule leçon, c'est la tienne,
fontaine, qui en toi-même retombes—
celle des eaux risquées auxquelles incombe
ce céleste retour vers la vie terrienne.

Autant que ton multiple murmure
rien ne saurait me servir d'exemple:
toi, ô colonne légère du temple
qui se détruit par sa propre nature.

Dans ta chute, combien se module
chaque jet d'eau qui termine sa danse.
Que je me sens l'élève, l'émule
de ton innombrable nuance!

Mais ce qui plus que ton chant vers toi me décide
c'est cet instant d'un silence en délire
lorsqu'à la nuit, à travers ton élan liquide
passe ton propre retour qu'un souffle retire.

25

We've forgotten so well
challenged gods and their rites,
that we envy faithful souls
their simple way of life.

It's not that we must please
nor that we must convert,
if we know to obey
the complementary orders.

26: THE FOUNTAIN

I want just one lesson, and it's yours,
fountain falling back into yourself—
that of risked waters on which depends
this celestial return toward earthly life.

Nothing will serve as example
as much as your multiple murmur:
you, O light column of a temple
that destroys itself by nature.

In your fall, how each jet of water
modulates itself as it ends its dance.
I feel like such a student, imitator
of your innumerable nuance.

But what's more convincing than your singing
is that instant of ecstatic silence when
at night, drawn back by a breath, your own
return passes through your liquid leaping.

27

Qu'il est doux parfois d'être de ton avis,
frere aîné, ô mon corps,
qu'il est doux d'être fort
de ta force,
de te sentir feuille, tige, écorce
et tout ce que tu peux devenir encore,
toi, si près de l'esprit.

Toi, si franc, si uni
dans ta joie manifeste
d'étre cet arbre de gestes
qui, un instant, ralentit
les allures célestes
pour y placer sa vie.

28: LA DÉESSE

Au midi vide qui dort
combien de fois elle passe,
sans laisser à la terrasse
le moindre soupçon d'un corps.

Mais si la nature la sent,
l'habitude de l'invisible
rend une clarté terrible
à son doux contour apparent.

29: VERGER

I

Peut-être que si j'ai osé t'écrire,
langue prêtée, c'était pour employer
ce nom rustique dont l'unique empire
me tourmentait depuis toujours: Verger.

27

Sometimes it's good to be
like you, older brother, O my body,
it's so good to be strong
with your strength,
to feel myself leaf, trunk, bark
and all else you still can become,
you, so close to spirit.

You, so free, so whole
in your obvious delight
to be this tree of gestures
which, one moment, slows down
that celestial pace,
and there situates its life.

28: THE GODDESS

In the empty sleeping noon,
how often she will pass
and not leave the slightest hint
of a body on the terrace.

But if nature senses her,
the habit of invisible power
renders a terrible clarity
to her soft visible contour.

29: THE ORCHARD

I

If I dared to write you, borrowed
tongue, perhaps it was to use
this rustic name whose rare kingdom
always has tormented me: Orchard.

Pauvre poéte qui doit élire
pour dire tout ce que ce nom comprend,
un à peu près trop vague qui chavire,
ou pire: la clôture qui défend.

Verger: ô privilège d'une lyre
de pouvoir te nommer simplement;
nom sans pareil qui les abeilles attire,
nom qui respire et attend. . . .

Nom clair qui cache le printemps antique,
tout aussi plein que transparent,
et qui dans ses syllabes symétriques
redouble tout et devient abondant.

II

Vers quel soleil gravitent
tant de désirs pesants?
De cette ardeur que vous dites,
où est le firmament?

Pour l'un à l'autre nous plaire,
faut-il tant appuyer?
Soyons légers et légères
à la terre remuée
par tant de forces contraires.

Regardez bien le verger:
c'est inévitable qu'il pèse;
pourtant de ce même malaise
il fait le bonheur de l'été.

III

Jamais la terre n'est plus réelle
que dans tes branches, ô verger blond,
ni plus flottante que dans la dentelle
que font tes ombres sur le gazon.

Poor poet, who must select
to say all that your name implies,
a vague approximate capsized,
or worse: a fence that protects.

Orchard: O lyre's privilege
to be able just to name you simply;
unequaled name attracting bees,
name that waits and breathes. . . .

Bright name hiding antique spring,
as much transparent as it's full,
which in its symmetry of syllables
becomes abundant by redoubling all.

II

Toward what sun do so many
heavy longings gravitate?
Where is the firmament
of this ardor you profess?

Just to please each other
must we lean so much?
Let us be light and lighter
on this earth that's moved
by such contrary powers.

Look closely at the orchard:
inevitably, it's heavy;
yet with the same malaise
it makes the summer happy.

III

Never is the earth more real
than in your branches, O blonde
orchard, nor more floating than
in your shade's lace on the lawn.

Là se rencontre ce qui nous reste,
ce qui pèse et ce qui nourrit
avec le passage manifeste
de la tendresse infinie.

Mais à ton centre, la calme fontaine,
presque dormant en son ancien rond,
de ce contraste parle à peine,
tant en elle il se confond.

IV

De leur grâce, que font-ils,
tous ces dieux hors d'usage,
qu'un passé rustique engage
à être sages et puérils?

Comme voilés par le bruit
des insectes qui butinent,
ils arrondissent les fruits
(occupation divine).

Car aucun jamais ne s'efface,
tant soit-il abandonné;
ceux qui parfois nous menacent
sont des dieux inoccupés.

V

Ai-je des souvenirs, ai-je des espérances,
    en te regardant, mon verger?
Tu te repais autour de moi, ô troupeau d'abondance,
    et tu fais penser ton berger.

Laisse-moi contempler au travers de tes branches
    la nuit qui va commencer.
Tu as travaillé; pour moi c'était un dimanche—
    mon repos, m'a-t-il avancé?

There, what is left for us,
what is heavy and what feeds
meets the manifest passage
of infinite tenderness.

But in your center, the calm fountain,
almost sleeping in her ancient round,
barely mentions contradictions,
since in her they're so well blended.

IV

What do they do with their wiles,
all these gods now out of usage
that a rustic past engages
to be wise and puerile?

As if veiled by the sound
of looting insects,
they make the fruit get round
(a divine occupation).

For none ever self-destructs,
no matter how abandoned;
and those who menace us
are gods now unemployed.

V

Do I have memories, do I have any hopes
      when I look at you, my orchard?
You feed yourself around me, O flock of abundance,
      and you make your shepherd think.

Through your branches let me contemplate
      the night about to start.
You have worked; for me it was a Sunday—
      did my rest do me any good?

D'être berger, qu'y a-t-il de plus juste en somme?
    Se peut-il qu'un peu de ma paix
aujourd'hui soit entrée doucement dans tes pommes?
    Car tu sais bien, je m'en vais. . . .

VI

N'était-il pas, ce verger, tout entier,
ta robe claire, autour de tes épaules?
Et n'as-tu pas senti combien console
son doux gazon qui pliait sous ton pied?

Que de fois, au lieu de promenade,
il s'imposait en devenant tout grand;
et c'était lui et l'heure qui s'évade
qui passaient par ton être hésitant.

Un livre parfois t'accompagnait. . . .
Mais ton regard, hanté de concurrences,
au miroir de l'ombre poursuivait
un jeu changeant de lentes ressemblances.

VII

Heureux verger, tout tendu à parfaire
de tous ses fruits les innombrables plans,
et qui sait bien son instinct séculaire
plier à la jeunesse d'un instant.

Quel beau travail, quel ordre que le tien!
Qui tant insiste dans les branches torses,
mais qui enfin, enchanté de leur force,
déborde dans un calme aérien.

Tes dangers et les miens, ne sont-ils point
tout fraternels, ô verger, ô mon frère?
Un même vent, nous venant de loin,
nous force d'être tendres et austères.

What could be better than to be a shepherd?
   Can it be that part of my peace
today has softly entered in your apples?
   For you well know that I am leaving. . . .

VI

This orchard, all of it, wasn't it
bright clothes around your shoulders?
And didn't you feel how much its soft
grass, that bent under foot, consoles?

How often, instead of parading,
it was impressive just by becoming great;
it was the orchard and evasive hour
that passed by your hesitant being.

Sometimes a book was with you. . . .
But, haunted by concurrences, your gaze
chased a changing game of slow resemblances
in the mirror of the shade.

VII

Happy orchard, stretched out to perfect
the countless plans of all your fruit,
and who well knows your daily instinct
bending toward an instant's youth.

What handsome work, what order is like yours!
So insistent in the twisted limbs,
but finally, enchanted by their power,
soars into an aerial calm.

Your dangers and my own, are they not
related, O orchard, O my brother?
The same wind, coming from afar,
forces us to be austere and tender.

30

Toutes les joies des aïeux
ont passé en nous et s'amassent;
leur cœur, ivre de chasse,
leur repos silencieux

devant un feu presque éteint. . . .
Si dans les instants arides
de nous notre vie se vide,
d'eux nous restons tout pleins.

Et combien de femmes ont dû
en nous se sauver, intactes,
comme dans l'entr'acte
d'une pièce qui n'a pas plu—

parées d'un malheur qu'aujourd'hui
personne ne veut ni ne porte,
elles paraissent fortes
appuyées sur le sang d'autrui.

Et des enfants, des enfants!
Tous ceux que le sort refuse,
en nous exercent la ruse
d'exister pourtant.

31: PORTRAIT INTÉRIEUR

Ce ne sont pas des souvenirs
qui, en moi, t'entretiennent;
tu n'es pas non plus mienne
par la force d'un beau désir.

30

All of our ancestors' pleasures
pass through us and amass;
their heart, wild with the hunt,
their taciturn rest

near a fire almost out. . . .
If, during arid moments,
our life spills out of us,
we remain still filled with them.

And how many women must have
escaped in us, intact,
as during the entr'acte
of a play that did not please—

dressed in misery no one
wears or wants these days,
propped on the blood
of others, they seem strong.

And the children, the children!
All those refused by fate,
in us they can pretend
that somehow they exist.

31: INTERIOR PORTRAIT

You don't survive in me
because of memories;
nor are you mine because
of a lovely longing's strength.

Ce qui te rend présente,
c'est le détour ardent
qu'une tendresse lente
décrit dans mon propre sang.

Je suis sans besoin
de te voir apparaître;
il m'a suffi de naître
pour te perdre un peu moins.

32

Comment encore reconnaître
ce que fut la douce vie?
En contemplant peut-être
dans ma paume l'imagerie

de ces lignes et de ces rides
que l'on entretient
en fermant sur le vide
cette main de rien.

33

Le sublime est un départ.
Quelque chose de nous qui au lieu
de nous suivre, prend son écart
et s'habitue aux cieux.

La rencontre extrême de l'art
n'est-ce point l'adieu le plus doux?
Et la musique: ce dernier regard
que nous jetons nous-mêmes vers nous!

What does make you present
is the ardent detour
that a slow tenderness
traces in my blood.

I do not need
to see you appear;
being born sufficed for me
to lose you a little less.

32

How can I recognize again
what was *la douce vie?*
Perhaps by contemplating
in my palm the imagery

of these lines and
ridges we preserve
by closing this hand
of nothing on the void.

33

The sublime is a departure.
Instead of following, something
in us starts going its own way
and getting used to heavens.

Isn't art's extreme encounter
the tenderest farewell?
And music: that last glance
that we ourselves throw back at us!

34

Combien de ports pourtant, et dans ces ports
combien de portes, t'accueillant peut-être,
combien de fenêtres
d'où l'on voit ta vie et ton effort.

Combien de grains ailés de l'avenir
qui, transportés au gré de la tempête,
un tendre jour de fête
verront leur floraison t'appartenir.

Combien de vies qui toujours se répondent;
et par l'essor que prend ta propre vie
en étant de ce monde,
quel gros néant à jamais compromis.

35

N'est-ce pas triste que nos yeux se ferment?
On voudrait avoir les yeux toujours ouverts,
pour avoir vu, avant le terme,
tout ce que l'on perd.

N'est-il pas terrible que nos dents brillent?
Il nous aurait fallu un charme plus discret
pour vivre en famille
en ce temps de paix.

Mais n'est-ce pas le pire que nos mains se cramponnent,
dures et gourmandes?
Faut-il que des mains soient simples et bonnes
pour lever l'offrande!

34

And yet how many ports, and in those ports
how many portals welcome you, perhaps,
from how many windows
can be seen your life and effort.

How many of the future's winged grains,
carried by the mercy of the storm,
one tender day of celebration
will see their bloom belong to you.

How many lives always answering each other;
and in the flight your own life takes
by being in this world,
what huge nothing compromised forever.

35

Isn't it sad that our eyes close?
We'd want our eyes always open
to have seen, before the end,
all that we lose.

Isn't it terrible our teeth shine?
We would have needed charm far more
discreet to live together
in this peace-time.

But isn't it worse that our hands clamp,
greedy and hard?
Hands must be simple and good
to lift the offering!

36

Puisque tout passe, faisons
la mélodie passagère;
celle qui nous désaltère
aura de nous raison.

Chantons ce qui nous quitte
avec amour et art;
soyons plus vite
que le rapide départ.

37

Souvent au-devant de nous
l'âme-oiseau s'élance;
c'est un ciel plus doux
qui déjà la balance,

pendant que nous marchons
sous des nuées épaisses.
Tout en peinant, profitons
de son ardente adresse.

38

Vues des Anges, les cimes des arbres peut-être
sont des racines, buvant les cieux;
et dans le sol, les profondes racines d'un hêtre
leur semblent des faîtes silencieux.

Pour eux, la terre, n'est-elle point transparente
en face d'un ciel, plein comme un corps?
Cette terre ardente, où se lamente
auprès des sources l'oubli des morts.

36

Since everything must pass,
let us sing a passing song;
the one that's satisfying
will be so because of us.

Let us sing about whatever
leaves with love and art;
let us be faster still
than that rapid departure.

37

The soul-bird often
soars ahead of us;
it's a sweeter heaven
that already poises it,

while we just plod on
under thick clouds. Still,
grieving, let us profit
from its ardent skill.

38

The Angels' view: perhaps the tips of trees
are roots that drink the skies;
and in the earth the beech's deepest
roots look like silent summits.

For them, is not the earth transparent
against a sky full as a corpse?
This ardent earth where, near the springs,
the dead's oblivion laments.

39

Ô mes amis, vous tous, je ne renie
aucun de vous; ni même ce passant
qui n'était de l'inconcevable vie
qu'un doux regard ouvert et hésitant.

Combien de fois un être, malgré lui,
arrête de son œil ou de son geste
l'imperceptible fuite d'autrui,
en lui rendant un instant manifeste.

Les inconnus. Ils ont leur large part
à notre sort que chaque jour complète.
Précise bien, ô inconnue discrète,
mon cœur distrait, en levant ton regard.

40

Un cygne avance sur l'eau
tout entouré de lui-même,
comme un glissant tableau;
ainsi à certains instants
un être que l'on aime
est tout un espace mouvant.

Il se rapproche, doublé,
comme ce cygne qui nage,
sur notre âme troublée . . .
qui à cet être ajoute
la tremblante image
de bonheur et de doute.

39

O my friends, all of you, I renounce
none of you; not even that transient
who, from the inconceivable life, was
no more than a soft glance, open and hesitant.

How often, with an eye or gesture,
someone, despite himself, stops
the imperceptible flight of another
by paying attention to him a moment.

Strangers. They play large parts
in our fate that every day completes.
O discreet stranger, take good aim,
as you lift your gaze toward my distracted heart.

40

A swan swims on the water
surrounded by itself
like a gliding picture;
thus at certain moments
a being that we love
is utter space in motion.

Like this swimming swan,
doubled, it comes closer
on our troubled soul . . .
which to this being adds
the rippling image
of happiness and doubt.

41

Ô nostalgie des lieux qui n'étaient point
assez aimés à l'heure passagère,
que je voudrais leur rendre de loin
le geste oublié, l'action supplémentaire!

Revenir sur mes pas, refaire doucement
—et cette fois, seul—tel voyage,
rester à la fontaine davantage,
toucher cet arbre, caresser ce banc. . . .

Monter à la chapelle solitaire
que tout le monde dit sans intérêt;
pousser la grille de ce cimetière,
se taire avec lui qui tant se tait.

Car n'est-ce pas le temps où il importe
de prendre un contact subtil et pieux?
Tel était fort, c'est que la terre est forte;
et tel se plaint, c'est qu'on la connait peu.

42

Ce soir quelque chose dans l'air a passé
qui fait pencher la tête;
on voudrait prier pour les prisonniers
dont la vie s'arrête.
Et on pense à la vie arrêtée. . . .

À la vie qui ne bouge plus vers la mort
et d'où l'avenir est absent;
où il faut être inutilement fort
et triste, inutilement.

41

O longing for the places that weren't loved
enough during the passing hour,
that from afar I want to offer them
the added act and the forgotten gesture!

Retrace my steps—this time alone—
slowly make that journey over,
remain by the fountain longer,
touch that tree, caress this bench. . . .

Climb to the solitary chapel
we all mention without interest;
push the cemetery grill,
be quiet with one who is so quiet.

For hasn't it become essential
to make a subtle, pious contact?
That was strong, because the earth is strong;
and this laments, because we barely know it.

42

Tonight there was something in the air
that makes us bow our heads;
we want to pray for prisoners
for whom life stops.
And we think of life stopped. . . .

Of life no longer moving toward death
and of where the future's absent;
where one must be uselessly strong
and sad, uselessly.

Où tous les jours piétinent sur place,
où toutes les nuits tombent dans l'abîme,
et où la conscience de l'enfance intime
à ce point s'efface,

qu'on a le cœur trop vieux pour penser un enfant.
Ce n'est pas tant que la vie soit hostile,
mais on lui ment,
enfermé dans le bloc d'un sort immobile.

43

Tel cheval qui boit à la fontaine,
telle feuille qui en tombant nous touche,
telle main vide, ou telle bouche
qui nous voudrait parler et qui ose à peine—

autant de variations de la vie qui s'apaise,
autant de rêves de la douleur qui somnole:
ô que celui dont le cœur est à l'aise
cherche la créature et la console.

44: PRINTEMPS

I

Ô mélodie de la sève
qui dans les instruments
de tous ces arbres s'élève—
accompagne le chant
de notre voix trop brève.

C'est pendant quelques mesures
seulement que nous suivons
les multiples figures
de ton long abandon,
ô abondante nature.

Where all days are marking time,
where all nights fall into the abyss,
and where childhood's intimate awareness
effaces itself at that point

when our heart's too old to think a child.
It's not so much that life is hostile,
but that we lie to it,
locked in a block of immobilized fate.

43

This horse drinking at the fountain,
this leaf touching us as it falls,
this empty hand, this mouth that wants
to speak to us but barely dares—

all signs of life that is appeased,
all dreams of a sleep-walking pain:
oh, let the one whose heart's at ease
search for and console creation.

44: SPRING

I

O melody of sap rising
in the instruments
of all these trees—
accompany the song
of our too-brief voice.

In only just a few
measures can we follow
the multiple strains
of your long abandon,
O abundant nature.

Quand il faudra nous taire,
d'autres continueront. . . .
Mais à présent comment faire
pour te rendre mon
grand cœur complémentaire?

II

Tout se prépare et va
vers la joie manifeste;
la terre et tout le reste
bientôt nous charmera.

Nous serons bien placés
pour tout voir, tout entendre;
on devra même se défendre
et parfois dire: assez!

Encore si on était dedans;
mais l'excellente place
est un peu trop en face
de ce jeu émouvant.

III

Montée des sèves dans les capillaires
qui tout à coup démontre aux vieillards
l'année trop raide qu'ils ne monteront guère
et qui en eux prépare le départ.

Leur corps (tout offensé par cet élan
de la nature brute qui ignore
que ces artères où elle bout encore
supportent mal un ordre impatient)

refuse la trop brusque aventure;
et pendant qu'il se raidit, méfiant,
pour subsister à sa façon, il rend
le jeu facile à la terre dure.

When we must be quiet,
others will continue. . . .
But now what can I do
to offer you my own
great contrapuntal heart?

II

Everything gets ready and moves
toward manifested joy;
the earth and all the rest
will soon be charming us.

We'll have places good enough
to see and to hear all;
we even should defend ourselves
and sometimes say: enough!

Still, if we were part of it;
but the very best place
is a little too face-
-to-face with this moving game.

III

The rise of sap in capillaries
that abruptly shows old men
the too-stiff year they'll hardly climb
and prepares departure in them.

Their bodies (offended by this thrust
of brute nature which ignores
that these arteries, where she still bubbles,
cannot endure an impatient order)

refuse this too-brusque adventure;
and, defiant, as they stiffen
to survive in her own way, they make
the game easy for the hard ground.

IV

C'est la sève qui tue
les vieux et ceux qui hésitent,
lorsque cet air insolite
flotte soudain dans les rues.

Tous ceux qui n'ont plus la force
de se sentir des ailes,
sont invités au divorce
qui à la terre les mêle.

C'est la douceur qui les perce
de sa pointe suprême,
et la caresse renverse
ceux qui résistent quand même.

V

Que vaudrait la douceur
si elle n'était capable,
tendre et ineffable,
de nous faire peur?

Elle surpasse tellement
toute la violence
que, lorsqu'elle s'élance,
nul ne se défend.

VI

En hiver, la mort meurtrière
entre dans les maisons;
elle cherche la sœur, le père,
et leur joue du violon.

Mais quand la terre remue
sous la bêche du printemps,
la mort court dans les rues
et salue les passants.

IV

Sap is what kills
the old and those who hesitate
when this insolent air
suddenly floats in the streets.

All those with no more
strength to walk on air
are called to the divorce
that mingles them with earth.

Sweetness pierces them
with its final sting,
and a caress topples
those who still resist.

V

Tender and ineffable,
what good would sweetness be
if it were never able
to frighten all of us?

It surpasses
violence so,
that when it springs
no one defends himself.

VI

In winter the murderer
death enters the house;
it looks for a sister, a father,
and fiddles for them.

But when the earth is moving
under the spade in spring,
death runs in the streets
and waves at the tourists.

VII

C'est de la côte d'Adam
qu'on a retiré Ève;
mais quand sa vie s'achève,
où va-t-elle, mourant?

Adam serait-il son tombeau?
Faut-il, lorsqu'elle se lasse,
lui ménager une place
dans un homme bien clos?

45

Cette lumière peut-elle
tout un monde nous rendre?
Est-ce plutôt la nouvelle
ombre, tremblante et tendre,
qui nous rattache à lui?
Elle qui tant nous ressemble
et qui tourne et tremble
autour d'un étrange appui.
Ombres des feuilles frêles,
sur le chemin et le pré:
geste soudain familier
qui nous adopte et nous mêle
à la trop neuve clarté.

46

Dans la blondeur du jour
passent deux chars pleins de briques:
ton rose qui revendique
et renonce tour à tour.

VII

Eve was drawn out
of Adam's side;
but when her life is lived,
where will she go to die?

Will Adam be her tomb?
When she grows exhausted,
must we manage room
for her in an airtight man?

45

Can such light offer
us an entire world?
Or is it the new shade,
trembling and tender,
that fastens us to it?
Shade that so resembles
us, that turns and trembles
round such a strange support.
Shades of fragile leaves,
on the meadow and the road:
sudden familiar gesture
that adopts and mingles
us with this too-new clarity.

46

Two wagons full of bricks
pass through the golden day:
a rose tone that asserts
and then, in turn, denies.

Comment se fait-il que soudain
ce ton attendri signifie
un nouveau complot de vie
entre nous et demain?

47

Le silence uni de l'hiver
est remplacé dans l'air
par un silence à ramage;
chaque voix qui accourt
y ajoute un contour,
y parfait une image.

Et tout cela n'est que le fond
de ce qui serait l'action
de notre cœur qui surpasse
le multiple dessin
de ce silence plein
d'inexprimable audace.

48

Entre le masque de brume
et celui de verdure,
voici le moment sublime où la nature
se montre davantage que de coutume.

Ah, la belle! Regardez son épaule
et cette claire franchise qui ose. . . .
Bientôt de nouveau elle jouera un rôle
dans la pièce touffue que l'été compose.

Why does this softened tone
signify so suddenly
a new conspiracy of life
between us and tomorrow?

47

Winter's total silence
in the air is supplanted
by a warbling silence;
each voice that joins in
adds a new dimension
and perfects a picture.

All that is but the start
of what will be the act
of our heart as it supplants
the multiple design
of this silence that is full
of unspeakable contempt.

48

Between the masques of mist and green
this is the sublime moment
when, more than customarily,
nature will reveal herself.

How gorgeous! Look at her shoulder
and that bright daring freedom. . . .
Soon she'll play her role again
in the bushy play composed by summer.

49: LE DRAPEAU

Vent altier qui tourmente le drapeau
dans la bleue neutralité du ciel,
jusqu'à le faire changer de couleur,
comme s'il voulait le tendre à d'autres nations
par-dessus les toits. Vent impartial,
vent du monde entier, vent qui relie,
évocateur des gestes qui se valent,
ô toi, qui provoques les mouvements interchangeables!
Le drapeau étale montre son plein écusson—
mais dans ses plis quelle universalité tacite!

Et pourtant quel fier moment
lorsqu'un instant le vent se déclare
pour tel pays: consent à la France,
ou subitement s'éprend
des Harpes légendaires de la verte Irlande.
Montrant toute l'image, comme un joueur de cartes
qui jette son atout,
et qui de son geste et de son sourire anonyme,
rappelle . . . je ne sais quelle image
de la Déesse qui change.

50: LA FENÊTRE

I

N'es-tu pas notre géométrie,
fenêtre, très simple forme
qui sans effort circonscris
notre vie énorme?

Celle qu'on aime n'est jamais plus belle
que lorsqu'on la voit apparaître
encadrée de toi; c'est, ô fenêtre,
que tu la rends presque éternelle.

49: THE FLAG

Haughty wind tormenting the flag
in the blue neutrality of sky,
even changing its color
as if offering it to other nations
over rooftops. Impartial wind,
wind of the whole world, uniting wind,
evoking worthy gestures,
O you, provoking interchangeable movements!
The unfurled flag reveals its full escutcheon—
but in its folds, what tacit universal!

And yet, how proud the moment
when the wind instantly declares itself
for a given country: consents to France
or is suddenly infatuated
with the legendary Harps of green Ireland.
Showing the whole picture, like a card player
who plays his trump
and who, with a gesture and anonymous smile,
recalls . . . I don't know what image
of the changing Goddess.

50: THE WINDOW

I

Aren't you our geometry,
window, very simple shape
circumscribing our enormous
life painlessly?

A lover's never so beautiful
as when we see her appear
framed by you; because, window,
you make her almost immortal.

Tous les hasards sont abolis. L'être
se tient au milieu de l'amour,
avec ce peu d'espace autour
dont on est maître.

II

Fenêtre, toi, ô mesure d'attente,
tant de fois remplie,
quand une vie se verse et s'impatiente
vers une autre vie.

Toi qui sépares et qui attires,
changeante comme la mer—
glace, soudain, où notre figure se mire
mêlée à ce qu'on voit à travers;

échantillon d'une liberté compromise
par la présence du sort;
prise par laquelle parmi nous s'égalise
le grand trop du dehors.

III

Assiette verticale qui nous sert
la pitance qui nous poursuit,
et la trop douce nuit
et le jour, souvent trop amer.

L'interminable repas,
assaisonné de bleu—
il ne faut pas être las
et se nourrir par les yeux.

Que de mets l'on nous propose
pendant que mûrissent les prunes;
ô mes yeux, mangeurs de roses,
vous allez boire de la lune!

All risks are cancelled. Being
stands at love's center,
with this narrow space around,
where we are master.

II

You, window, O waiting's measure,
refilled so often
when one life spills out and grows
impatient for another.

You who divides and attracts,
as fickle as the sea—
sudden mirror reflecting our face
mingled with what we see in back;

fraction of a freedom compromised
by the presence of risk;
trapped by whatever's in us
that evens the odds of the loaded outside.

III

Vertical plate serving us
the pittance that pursues
us, the night too tender
and day too often bitter.

Endless meal
seasoned with blue—
we just can't loll
and let our eyes feed us.

What menus are proposed
during the ripening of prunes;
O my eyes, devourers of roses,
you will drink the moon!

51

À la bougie éteinte,
dans la chambre rendue à l'espace,
on est frôlé par la plainte
de feu la flamme sans place.

Faisons-lui un subtil
tombeau sous notre paupière,
et pleurons comme une mère
son très familier péril.

52

C'est le paysage longtemps, c'est une cloche,
c'est du soir la délivrance si pure—
mais tout cela en nous prépare l'approche
d'une nouvelle, d'une tendre figure....

Ainsi nous vivons dans un embarras très étrange
entre l'arc lointain et la trop pénétrante flèche:
entre le monde trop vague pour saisir l'ange
et Celle qui, par trop de présence, l'empêche.

53

On arrange et on compose
les mots de tant de façons,
mais comment arriverait-on
à égaler une rose?

Si on supporte l'étrange
prétention de ce jeu,
c'est que, parfois, un ange
le dérange un peu.

51

When the candle has burned out,
in the room turned into space,
we're touched by the fire's moan,
a flame that's lost its place.

Let's make a subtle sepulchre
for it beneath our eyelid,
and, like a mother, weep
for its too-familiar danger.

52

It's the endless landscape, it's a bell,
it's that pure deliverance of night—
but in us, all that starts to signal
the coming of a new, a tender figure. . . .

Thus we live in a strange embarrassment
between a distant arc and too-penetrating arrow:
between a world too vague to hold the angel
and She who hinders it with too much presence.

53

We arrange and we compose
words in so many ways,
but when will we find ways
to be equal to the rose?

If we keep up the strange
pretension of this game,
it's because at times an angel
deranges it a little.

54

J'ai vu dans l'œil animal
la vie paisible qui dure,
le calme impartial
de l'imperturbable nature.

La bête connaît la peur;
mais aussitôt elle avance
et sur son champ d'abondance
broute une présence
qui n'a pas le goût d'ailleurs.

55

Faut-il vraiment tant de danger
à nos objets obscurs?
Le monde serait-il dérangé,
étant un peu plus sûr?

Petit flacon renversé,
qui t'a donné cette mince base?
De ton flottant malheur bercé,
l'air est en extase.

56: LA DORMEUSE

Figure de femme, sur son sommeil
fermée, on dirait qu'elle goûte
quelque bruit à nul autre pareil
qui la remplit toute.

De son corps sonore qui dort
elle tire la jouissance
d'être un murmure encore
sous le regard du silence.

54

In the animal eye I saw
a peaceable life that endures,
the unprejudiced calm
of dispassionate nature.

A beast knows what fear is
but keeps going nonetheless;
and in its field of plenty
a certain presence grazes
with no taste for someplace else.

55

Do our humble things
really need so much danger?
Would the world be deranged,
if it were a little surer?

Small spilled bottle,
who gave you that thin base?
Rocked by your floating casualty,
the air's in ecstasy.

56: SLEEPING WOMAN

Savoring sleep, the figure
of a woman seems to taste
a noise that's like no other
and that fills her up again.

From the echo of her sleeping
body, she draws the pleasure
of still being just a murmur
beneath the glance of silence.

57: LA BICHE

Ô la biche: quel bel intérieur
d'anciennes forêts dans tes yeux abonde;
combien de confiance ronde
mêlée à combien de peur.

Tout cela, porté par la vive
gracilité de tes bonds.
Mais jamais rien n'arrive
à cette impossessive
ignorance de ton front.

58

Arrêtons-nous un peu, causons.
C'est encore moi, ce soir, qui m'arrête,
c'est encore vous qui m'écoutez.

Un peu plus tard d'autres joueront
aux voisins sur la route
sous ces beaux arbres que l'on se prête.

59

Tous mes adieux sont faits. Tant de départs
m'ont lentement formé dès mon enfance.
Mais je reviens encore, je recommence,
ce franc retour libère mon regard.

Ce qui me reste, c'est de le remplir,
et ma joie toujours impénitente
d'avoir aimé des choses ressemblantes
à ces absences qui nous font agir.

57: THE DOE

Ah, the doe: what lovely hearts
of ancient woods abound inside your eyes;
so much total confidence
fused with so much fear.

All that, borne by the vibrance
of your graceful bounds.
But in your brow's
unpossessive ignorance
nothing ever happens.

58

Let's stop a while, let's talk.
Tonight, again, I am the one who stops
myself, you are the one who listens.

A little later, others will pretend
that they are neighbors on the road
under these lovely trees we lend ourselves.

59

All my goodbyes are said. Many separations
slowly shaped me since my infancy.
But I come back again and I begin again;
this fresh return releases my attention.

What's left for me is to replenish it,
and my joy, forever unrepentant
for having loved the things resembling
these absences that make us act.

Saltimbanques

POÈMES EN PROSE

Saltimbanques

PROSE POEMS

Saltimbanques

1

Notre chemin n'est pas plus large que le tien, souvent nous tombons de tout haut, aussi sommes-nous cassés, mais l'attention absente ne nous oblige point de remonter à la corde. Toi, ta moindre faute, te ferait mourir. Nous amusons de nos mille fautes une mort spectatrice qui occupe la meilleure place dans le cirque de nos malheurs.

2

Faisons comme eux: ne tombons jamais sans mourir. Quel attroupement autour de notre chute! Mais un enfant, un peu à l'écart, regarde la corde vide avec, derrière, la nuit intacte.

3

La corde était si haute, que cela se passait au-dessus des réflecteurs. Tout à l'heure elle était encore parmi nous dans son maillot trop rose. C'était un autre rose qui, là-haut, expliquait à la nuit immense l'absurdité de son pur danger mouvant.

4

Quelle perfection. Si c'était dans l'âme, quels saints vous feriez!—C'est dans l'âme, mais ils ne la touchent que par hasard, dans les rares moments d'une imperceptible maladresse.

Saltimbanques

1

Our road is no wider than yours. We often fall from up high. We're broken, too, but our lack of attention doesn't force us to climb the rope again. Your slightest mistake can kill you. Our thousand mistakes amuse death, that spectator with the best seat in our circus of pain.

2

Let's be like them: let's never fall without dying. Such a crowd around our plunge! But off a little to one side, a child looks at the empty rope with the night behind, intact.

3

The rope was so high, all of that happened above the spotlights. Later, it was back among us again in its too-pink tights. Up there it was another rose demonstrating to the immense night the absurdity of its pure moving danger.

4

Such perfection. If it were in your soul, what saints you'd make!—It *is* in your soul, but you feel it only by accident, in those rare moments of an awkward move that no one sees.

À Monique

un petit recueillement de ma gratitude

L'HEURE DU THÉ

Buvant dans cette tasse sur laquelle, dans une langue inconnue, sont peut-être inscrits des signes de bénédiction et de bonheur, je la tiens dans cette main pleine de lignes à son tour que je ne saurais expliquer. Sont-elles d'accord ces deux écritures, et puisqu'elles sont seules entre elles et toujours secrètes sous la coupole de mon regard, vont-elles dialoguer à leur façon et se concilier, ces deux textes millénaires qu'un geste de buveur rapproche?

CHAPELLE RUSTIQUE

Comme la maison est calme: écoute! Mais, là-haut, dans la blanche chapelle, d'où vient ce surcroît de silence?—De tous ceux qui depuis plus d'un siècle y sont entrés pour ne pas être dehors, et qui, en s'agenouillant, se sont effrayés de leur bruit? De cet argent qui, en tombant dans le tronc, a perdu sa voix et qui n'aura qu'un petit bruissement de grillon quand il sera recueilli? Ou de cette douce absence de Sainte-Anne, patronne du sanctuaire, qui n'ose pas approcher, pour ne pas abîmer cette pure distance que suppose un appel?

For Monique

a small gathering of my gratitude

TEATIME

While drinking from this cup perhaps inscribed with signs of blessing and of happiness in an unknown tongue, I hold it in this hand full of its own lines I can never explain. Do these two scripts agree? And since they are alone and secluded inside the dome of my glance, will they speak to one another in their own way and be reconciled, these two ancient texts a drinker's gesture brings together?

RUSTIC CHAPEL

How calm the house is: listen! But up there in the white chapel, where does that greater silence come from?—From all those who, for more than a century, came in simply not to be outdoors and, kneeling down, frightened themselves with their own noise? From the money that lost its voice as it fell in the collection box and will make a little cricket's noise when it is gathered? Or from this sweet absence of Saint Anne, the sanctuary's patron, who doesn't dare come closer, afraid to spoil that pure distance a call implies?

«FARFALLETTINA»

Toute agitée elle arrive vers la lampe, et son vertige lui donne un dernier répit confus avant d'être brûlée. Elle s'est abattue sur le vert tapis de la table, et sur ce fond avantageux s'étale pour un instant (pour une durée à elle que nous ne saurions mesurer) le luxe de son inconcevable splendeur. On dirait, en trop petit, une dame qui avait une panne en se rendant au Théâtre. Elle n'y arrivera point. Et d'ailleurs où est le Théâtre pour de si frêles spectateurs...? Ses ailes dont on aperçoit les minuscules baguettes d'or remuent comme un double éventail devant nulle figure; et, entre elles, ce corps mince, bilboquet où sont retombés deux yeux en boule d'émeraude....

C'est en toi, ma belle, que Dieu s'est épuisé. Il te lance à la flamme pour regagner un peu de sa force. (Comme un enfant qui casse sa tirelire.)

LE MANGEUR DE MANDARINES

Oh, quelle prévoyance! Ce lapin entre les fruits. Pense! Trente-sept petits noyaux dans un seul exemplaire prêts à tomber un peu partout et à faire progéniture. Il a fallu que nous corrigions ça. Elle eût été capable de peupler la terre cette petite Mandarine entêtée qui porte une robe si large comme si elle devait encore grandir. Mal habillée en somme; plus occupée de multiplication que de mode. Montre-lui la grenade dans son armure de cuir de Cordoue: elle éclate d'avenir, se retient, dédaigne....

Et laissant entrevoir sa lignée possible, elle l'étouffe dans un berceau de pourpre. La terre lui semble trop évasive pour faire avec elle un pacte d'abondance.

"FARFALLETTINA"

Shaking all over, she arrives near the lamp and her dizziness grants her one last confused reprieve before she burns up. She's fallen on the green tablecloth, and on that advantageous background she stretches out the luxuriousness of her inconceivable splendor a moment (a span of her time we will never learn to measure). She looks like a miniature woman who has collapsed on her way to the Theater. She'll never get there. Besides, where is there Theater for such a fragile audience . . . ? We notice tiny gold threads in her wings moving like a double fan in front of no one's face; between them this thin body, a toy tumbler in which the emerald balls of two eyes fell. . . .

My dear, God exhausted himself in you. He tosses you into the fire to regain a bit of his strength. (Like a boy breaking his bank.)

TANGERINE EATER

Oh, what foresight! This rabbit of the fruit-world. Imagine, in a single specimen thirty-seven small seeds ready to fall just about anywhere and sprout her progeny. We had to fix that. She could have populated the earth—this little determined Mandarin who wears an oversized dress as if she were to grow bigger. In fact, badly dressed: more preoccupied with multiplication than with style. Show her the pomegranate in her armor of Cordova leather: she is exploding with future, controls herself, conde-scends. . . . And revealing a glimpse of her possible offspring, she suffo-cates them in a crimson cradle. The earth seems too evasive to enter a pact of abundance with her.

(Poème en Prose)

Beau paysage, brodé de verdure, étalé ce soir, comme une belle étoffe que le marchand fait valoir.

Petite déesse qui se recache constamment sous son manteau d'eau.

Oiseaux qui passent comme une pensée.

Pays à la figure tragique, les ombres des nuages s'y sont mêlées pour le former.

Mais la clarté verte des alpages qui les fait appartenir au ciel, plus qu'à la rude montagne dont ils forment les pentes entre l'obscurité des sapins.

Mais dans ce ciel les trouées d'un bleu sublimement éloigné, d'un bleu infini.

Et à l'ouest, derrière d'autres nuages, le coucher d'un soleil violent qui semble se briser dans son trop brusque départ.

Et toujours, en face de moi, la petite déesse d'eau qui se défait et renaît sous sa chute. L'écume de sa pudeur, et l'onde qui lui fait une épaule innombrable.

La grisaille d'un saule au-dessus d'elle, et un églantier aux gestes d'abondance et qui a longtemps fleuri.

(Melon)

Comment fais-tu, beau melon, d'être si frais à l'intérieur, après avoir eu tout ce soleil pour mûrir? Cela me rappelle l'amante délicieuse qui avait des lèvres de source, même au plus fort de l'été de l'amour.

Mélancolie Matinale

Tout semblait déjà sec et brûlé à ce commencement de jour qui, sans doute, sera gris et torride. Seules les feuilles mortes d'été, roulées par terre, avaient conservé la rosée.

(Prose Poem)

Gorgeous landscape embroidered green, stretched out tonight like beautiful material displayed by a merchant.

Small goddess always hiding herself under her gold cape.

Birds passing like a thought.

Country with a tragic face shaped by shadows of shifting clouds.

But the pastures' bright green light makes them belong to the sky more than to the rugged Alps whose slopes they carve in the darkness of pines.

But in the sky, gaps of a sublimely distant blue, an infinite blue.

And in the West, behind more clouds, the violent sunset seems to break because it is leaving too fast.

And always facing me, the little water goddess who demolishes and restores herself in her fall. Her modesty's foam and the spray magnifying her shoulder.

Above her, a willow's grisaille and the overflowing gestures of a wild rose that has bloomed too long.

(Melon)

Beautiful melon, how can you be so cool inside after needing so much sun to ripen? You remind me of a delicious lover whose lips were springs even during love's hottest summer.

Morning Melancholy

Everything seemed already dry and burnt at the start of this day that no doubt will be gray and torrid. Only summer's leaves, curled up on the ground, had conserved the dew.

Cimetière

Y en a-t-il d'arrière goût de la vie dans ces tombes? Et les abeilles,
trouvent-elles dans la bouche des fleurs un presque-mot qui se tait? Ô
fleurs, prisonnières de nos instincts de bonheur, revenez-vous vers nous
avec nos morts dans les veines? Comment échapper à notre emprise,
fleurs? Comment ne pas être *nos* fleurs? Est-ce de tous ces pétales que la
rose s'éloigne de nous? Veut-elle être rose-seule, rien-que-rose? Sommeil
de personne sous tant de paupières?

Cemetery

Is there an aftertaste of life in these graves? And in the flowers' mouths do bees find the hint of a word refusing speech? O flowers, prisoners of our instincts to be happy, do you come back to us with our dead in your veins? Flowers, how can you escape our grip? How can you not be *our* flowers? Does the rose use all its petals to fly away from us? Does it want to be only a rose, nothing but rose? No one's sleep under so many eyelids?

Migration des Forces

The Migration of Powers

for

MICHEL GAULIN

mon semblable, mon cher frère

Ça semblait un moment avant tant d'autres
et c'était tout, mon Dieu, et tellement nôtre
et c'était trop et nous étions trop peu!
———R. M RILKE

(L'Enfant à la Fenêtre)

L'enfant, à la fenêtre, attend le retour de sa mère.
C'est l'heure lente où son être s'altère
d'attente illimitée. . . .
Comment suffire à son doux regard préliminaire
qui partout ne voit que ce qui diffère
de l'unique maternité?
Ces vagues passants que son attente nivelle
ont-ils tort, dites, de ne pas être celle
qui tant suffit . . . ?

Les Fugitifs

Restons au bord de cette route sombre,
arrêtez-vous, attendons, mon enfant!
Autour de nous les périls sont sans nombre
et nous sommes seuls, les outrageant.

—Un chant! Un chant!

Comment chanter dans ce noir si vide,
offrir un son à ce néant, comment?
Ne sens-tu pas la nuit enfanticide
qui guette tout ce qui paraît naissant?

—Un chant! Un chant!

Chanter? Quoi?—Cet être qui renonce,
l'indifférence de ce demi-vent?
Les pierres qui nous faisaient mal? Les ronces?
Ce traître chemin sous ce pied vacillant?

—Un chant, un chant!

(Child at the Windowsill)

The child at the windowsill waits for his mother's
return. This is that slow hour when his whole being
is transformed by endless waiting. . . .
What can satisfy his soft preliminary glance
which all around him sees only what differs
from the unrivaled motherhood?
These vague passersby levelled by his vigil,
are they at fault, say, for not being her
who satisfies so much. . . ?

The Fugitives

Let's stay by the side of this dark road,
stop here, and let us wait, my child!
There are countless dangers all around
us, and we, the violated, are alone.

—A song! A song!

How can I sing in such an empty dark,
how can I offer one sound to this void?
Don't you feel this infanticidal night
watching all that appears to be born?

—A song! A song!

Sing? What?—This being who disowns,
the indifference of this demi-wind?
The rocks that hurt us, and the thorns?
This treacherous road under our unsteady feet?

—A song, a song!

Eh bien, je chanterai dans ton oreille.
Et ce sera ce mince voilier
que l'on construit dedans une bouteille
avec ses mâts et vergues, tout entier,

qui restera dans ton cœur transparent.

Chat

Chat d'étalage, âme qui confère
à tant d'objets épars son rêve lent,
et qui se prête, en conscience-mère,
à tout un monde inconscient.

Silence chaud et fauve, qui s'impose
à ce mutisme mutilé,
et qui remplit l'orphelinat des choses
d'un fier dédain à être caressé. . . .

Elle s'endort d'un air si intégral
entre cristaux, fayences et dorures,
que le dessin plaintif de leurs fêlures
semble signé d'un malheur magistral.

Enterrement

Parmi les machines rapides
qui, agacées et rapaces,
traversent le nouveau-vide
de l'indomptable espace,
passe la lente limace d'un enterrement. . . .

Mais les astres sont plus lents.

Well then, I'll sing something in your ear.
And it will be a fragile sailing ship
constructed in a bottle,
complete with all its masts and sails,

that will remain inside your own transparent heart.

Cat

The show cat: a soul conferring
its slow dream on all those scattered objects,
and in primal consciousness bestowing
itself to a whole unconscious world.

Warm and musky silence imposing
itself on the mutilated muteness
and filling the orphanage of things
with a proud disdain for being caressed. . . .

Among the crystals, fayences, and gilts,
she sleeps with such an integral air
that the plaintive pattern of their cracks
seems signed by magisterial misfortune.

Funeral

Among the fast machines
which, rapacious and annoyed,
cross the new-made void
of unconquerable space,
passes the slow slug of a funeral. . . .

But the stars are slower still.

Doute

Tendre nature, nature heureuse, où tant
de désirs se recherchent et s'entrecroisent,
indifférente, et pourtant base
des consentements,

nature trop pleine où se détruit et déchire
ce qui s'exalte trop tôt,
où de la rivalité du délicieux et du pire
naît un semblant de repos,

nature, tueuse par son excès, créatrice,
toujours extasiée,
qui réchauffes et qui consumes le vice
sur un même brasier:

Dis-moi, silencieuse, ô dis-moi, suis-je
comme un instant de tes fruits?
Fais-je partie de l'abîme de ton vertige
où se jettent tes nuits?

Suis-je d'accord avec tes desseins ineffables?
Serais-je de tes révoltes un cri?
Moi, qui fus pain, suis-je tombé de la table,
miette perdue qui durcit?

Doubt

Tender nature, happy nature, where so many
desires seek and intersect each other,
indifferent, and yet still the basis
of consents,

overflowing nature where what exalts itself
too soon lacerates and destroys itself,
where from the rivalry of the delicious and the worst
is born some semblance of repose,

nature, killer by excess, creator,
always ecstatic,
that rekindles and consumes evil
on the same brazier:

Tell me, silencer, O tell me, am I
like an instant of your fruits?
Am I part of your dizzying abyss
where your nights hurl themselves?

Am I in harmony with your ineffable designs?
Will I become a shout of your revolts?
I, who was bread, have I fallen from the table,
a lost crumb turning hard?

Source

Parle, ô source, toi qui n'es pas humaine;
chante, ô source, tes pleurs!
Rien ne console autant de la trop indigène peine
qu'une peine d'ailleurs.

Est-ce de la peine, ton chant? Ô dis-moi, est-ce
quelque état inconnu?
En dehors de ce qui nous aide et ce qui nous blesse
peut-on être ému?

Mouvement de Rêve

Ascenseur, qui parcourt sans bruit les étages du rêve,
monte, s'arrête et redescend,
doux départ, arrêt bref, brève trêve
qui se charge de changements. . . .

De la lenteur dans une pilule
qui en fondant approfondit
cette fuite qui dissimule
le désir inassouvi

de rester, de trouver le centre
où se jouent soleil et rosée,
et de ne plus, surtout, de ne plus choisir entre
les malheurs identiques et les cœurs opposés.

Spring

O spring, you who aren't human, speak;
sing your cries, O spring!
Nothing so consoles that too inner pain
than pain from somewhere else.

Does your song come from pain? Oh,
tell me, is it some unknown state?
Can we be moved by anything, except
by what helps and by what wounds us?

Dream Movement

Elevator, moving through the stories of the dream
noiselessly, ascends, stops, and descends again,
soft start, brusque stop, brief truce
that charges itself with changes. . . .

With the slowness in a pill
which, while melting, deepens
this flight that dissembles
the unsatisfied desire

to remain, to discover the center
where dew and sunlight are at play,
and never, especially, never again to choose
between identical disasters and opposite hearts.

Disgrâce Divine

Ce ne sera plus par vous, bouche trop infidèle,
que parlera ma brusque volonté;
je vous ai éprouvée, mais votre souffle mêle
tous les hasards du cœur à ma dictée.

S'il y aura douceur, ce ne sera que la vôtre:
arrière-goût sucré, salive coloriée,
séduisant tout un peu, vite affadie . . . autre
que mon miel en moi multiplié.

Désormais ce sera vous, rigueur ou amertume,
vous seules, qui sonnerez sous d'innombrables coups:
car je suis le marteau, et vous restez l'enclume,
mais plus de fer à forger entre nous!

Hiver

J'aime les hivers d'autrefois qui n'étaient point encore sportifs.
On les craignait un peu, tant ils étaient durs et vifs;
on les affrontait avec un brin de courage,
pour rentrer chez soi, blanc, étincelant, roi-mage.
Et le feu, ce grand feu qui nous consolait d'eux,
était un feu fort et vivant, un vrai feu.
On écrivait mal, on avait les doigts tout raides,
mais quelle joie de rêver et d'entretenir ce qui aide
aux souvenirs qui s'en vont, de tarder un peu. . . .
Il venaient si près, on les voyait mieux
qu'en été . . . on leur proposait des couleurs.
Tout était peinture à l'intérieur,
tandis que dehors tout se faisait estampe.

Et les arbres, qui travaillaient chez eux, à la lampe. . . .

Divine Disgrace

Too unfaithful mouth, my blunt will
shall never speak through you again;
I tried you out, but your breath scrambles
my dictation with all the hazards of the heart.

If there is tenderness, it will be yours alone:
sugary aftertaste, colored saliva,
seducing everything a little, quickly insipid . . .
anything but the honey multiplied in me.

From now on it shall be you, harshness or bitterness,
you alone shall ring under numberless blows:
for I am the hammer and you remain the anvil,
but no more iron forged between us!

Winter

I love those former winters that still weren't meant for sports.
We feared them a little, they were so hard and sharp;
we confronted them with a bit of courage,
to return into our house, white, sparkling wise-men.
And the fire, that great fire consoling us against them,
was a strong and living fire, a real fire.
We wrote badly, our fingers were all stiff,
but what joy to dream and entertain whatever
helps escaping memories delay a while. . . .
They came so close, we saw them better
than in summer . . . we proposed colors to them.
Inside, all was painting,
while outside all became engraving.

And the trees, who worked at home, in lamplight. . . .

Solitude

De tendresses pleines, les mains,
et nul qui ferait la vendange!
Faut-il crier aux anges?

Hélas! Notre trop-plein
devant eux devient indigence.
Notre appel qui s'élance
n'est qu'un bruyant voisin
de l'indifférence.

Vieillir

Certains étés il y a tant de fruits
que les paysans ne daignent plus les prendre.
Aije, moi, ô vous, mes jours, mes nuits,
sans récolter, laissé passer aux cendres
les lentes flammes de vos beaux produits?

Mes nuits, mes jours, vous avez tant porté!
Vos branches toutes ont gardé le geste
du long labeur dont vous sortez:
mes jours, mes nuits, ô mes amis agrestes!

Je cherche ce qui tant vous fut propice.
Douceur pareille, pourrait-elle encore,
ô mes beaux arbres presque morts,
flatter vos feuilles, ouvrir un calice?

Ah, plus de fruits! Mais une fois dernière
s'épanouir en vaine floraison,
sans réfléchir, sans compter, comme font
inutilement les forces millénaires.

Solitude

Hands filled with tenderness,
and nothing to be harvested!
Must we cry out to angels?

But, ah! Before them our
surplus becomes indigence.
And our rising call
is nothing but the noisy
neighbor of indifference.

Growing Old

In some summers there is so much fruit,
the peasants decide not to reap anymore.
Not having reaped you, O my days,
my nights, have I let the slow flames
of your lovely produce fall into ashes?

My nights, my days, you have borne so much!
All your branches have retained the gesture
of that long labor you are rising from:
my days, my nights. O my rustic friends!

I look for what was so good for you.
O my lovely, half-dead trees,
could some equal sweetness still
stroke your leaves, open your calyx?

Ah, no more fruit! But one last time
bloom in fruitless blossoming,
without planning, without reckoning,
as uselessly as the powers of millennia.

Bulles de Savon

Oh, les bulles de savon!
Quel ancien souvenir de dimanche.
Leur vide prend sa revanche
en confectionnant ces fruits ronds

du néant. D'être lancé
un peu de souffle se flatte.
Et comme ces bulles éclatent
lorsqu'elles commencent à penser.

Qui ne serait pas plein
d'une tendre insouciance
voyant nous quitter d'aisance
ces soupirs qui se lavent les mains?

(Cytise et Citronnelle)

C'est vous, Cytise et Citronnelle,
qui me faites encore sentir mon enfance.
Ô des étés la longue chance
sûre, lente et mutuelle.
C'est toi, mon cœur en permanence,
que je réclame aux fugitives
choses, à ces ombres vives
qui traversent mes attirances.

Soap Bubbles

Oh, soap bubbles!
Memories of Sundays long ago:
their emptiness takes its revenge
by fabricating these round fruits

of nothingness. A bit of breath
boasts of being launched.
And just as they start
to think, these bubbles burst.

Who would not be filled
with a tender carelessness,
seeing with what ease they leave us,
these sighs that wash their hands?

(Lemon and Laburnum)

It's still you, lemon and laburnum,
that make me feel my childhood.
O the long fate of those summers,
sure, slow and mutual.
It's you, my constant heart,
that I reclaim in fugitive
things, in these vivid shadows
moving in my spheres of influence.

(Femme devant Sa Glace)

Entre elle et sa glace,
grâce à son cœur pensif,
il naît un peu d'espace
légèrement portatif
qui presque lui appartient.

Ce subtil va-et-vient
d'une inépuisable image
fait à son regard aérien
une cage.

C'est là, peut-être, qu'il chante
sa clarté la plus pure.
Seul. Pour prendre mesure
de la liberté provocante.

(Mentir à un Enfant)

Pourquoi tant te mentir, ô enfant, dans ton doux nid initial?
À peine que tu opposeras à cette caresse pleine
un peu de ton propre toi . . . le consentement animal
aura vite cédé à l'envie de la dureté humaine.

Ce n'est du terrible amour que la première emprise;
il prend tes mesures, déjà il te juge, l'amour:
bientôt il entourera ta douce confiance conquise
de son inexorable contour!

(Woman at Her Mirror)

Because of her pensive heart,
between her and her mirror
a small, slightly portable
space that almost belongs
to her begins to grow.

This subtle coming and going
of an inexhaustible image
constructs a cage
for her airy glance.

There, perhaps, it sings
its purest clarity.
Alone. To measure
provocative freedom.

(Lying to a Child)

Why lie to you so much, O child, in your first soft nest?
As soon as you'll oppose this full embrace
a little with your own proper self . . . the animal consent
shall have surrendered quickly to the will of human hardness.

This is just the first mastery of terrifying love;
love measures you, it already judges you:
soon it will surround your soft conquered confidence
with its own inexorable contour!

(L'Ensemble Silent)

À quoi donc mesure-t-on
ce qui passe et, tour à tour,
semble trop long ou trop court
à l'imprévisible saison
de nos cœurs peu utilisables?
N'importe que vous dormez
ou que vous vous mettez à table,
on finit par se conformer
à l'inénarrable.
Quel silence autour de nos vies,
malgré tel mot qui voudrait
vivre. On pleure, on crie,
mais l'ensemble se tait.

À la Lune

Lune, svelte personne,
qui est celui qui te donne
chaque mois un enfant?
Et qui te rend sans cesse
occupée de ta grossesse
presque terrestrement?

Tu attires le sang
de nos vierges pubères.
Mais de quoi es-tu mère
douze fois par an?

Élèverions-nous en nous
ta légère progéniture?
J'ai trouvé en moi un doux
berceau orné de dorures,
qui me paraît de ton goût.

(The Silent Whole)

Against what, then, do we measure
whatever happens and, in turn,
seems too long or too short
for the unpredictable season
of our barely useable hearts?
Whether we are sleeping
or just sitting at the table,
we end up by conforming
to the unutterable.
Such silence around our lives,
despite this word that wants
to live. We cry, we shout,
but the whole says nothing.

To the Moon

Moon, svelte person,
who makes you pregnant
every month?
And who makes you always
engrossed in your pregnancy
—almost terrestrially?

You attract the blood
of our pubescent virgins.
But what do you mother
twelves times a year?

Shall we raise your light
offspring in ourselves?
Inside me I found a soft
cradle decorated with gilt
which I think suits your taste.

Nénuphar

J'ai toute ma vie, mais qui la dirait mienne
me priverait, car elle est infinie.
Le frisson d'eau, la teinte aérienne
sont à moi; c'est encore cela, ma vie.

Aucun désir ne m'ouvre: je suis pleine,
jamais je ne me referme par refus—
au rythme de mon âme quotidienne
je ne désire point—je suis émue;

par ce mouvement j'exerce mon empire,
rendant réels les rêves du soir
car à mon corps du fond de l'eau j'attire
les au-delà des miroirs. . . .

(Ce Qui Dure)

Qui nous dit que tout disparaisse?
De l'Oiseau que tu blesses,
qui sait, s'il ne reste le vol,
et peut-être les fleurs des caresses
survivent à nous, à leur sol.

Ce n'est pas le geste qui dure
mais il vous revêt de l'armure
d'or—des seins jusqu'aux genoux—
et tant la bataille fut pure
qu'un Ange la porte après vous.

Water Lily

My whole life is mine, but whoever says so
will deprive me, for it is infinite.
The ripple of water, the shade of the sky
are mine; it is still the same, my life.

No desire opens me: I am full,
I never close myself with refusal—
in the rhythm of my daily soul
I do not desire—I am moved;

by being moved I exert my empire,
making the dreams of night real:
into my body at the bottom of the water
I attract the beyonds of mirrors. . . .

(What Survives)

Who says that all must vanish?
Who knows, perhaps the flight
of the bird you wound remains,
and perhaps flowers survive
caresses in us, in their ground.

It isn't the gesture that lasts,
but it dresses you again in gold
armor—from breast to knees—
and the battle was so pure
an Angel wears it after you.

Cimetière à Flaach

Tombeaux, tombeaux, debout comme des personnes
dans cet enclos en vain fermé,
cet air si tendre qui vous environne
et tout autour de vous, heureux, ce pré

ne vous font-ils regretter au moins
en ce moment, ô pierres indifférentes,
le sort d'antan quand vous étiez un coin
vivant pourtant de la montagne vivante?

Quel lot funeste vous attache aux morts
qui malgré vous s'évadent et se mêlent
aux changements, tandis que vous encore
imitez leur raideur, horribles stèles?

Ossuaire

N'y a-t-il plus que des Victoires
aux ailes cassées?
Et l'amour laisse-t-il toujours choire
les enlacés?

Qui les rappelle, les sources mortes
et les sourires?
Et cette onde qui nous emporte—
c'est vers le pire.

On voudrait, pour que rien ne se passe
qu'on nous arrête.
Mais la mort qui se presse, entasse
tête sur tête.

Cemetery in Flaach

Tombstones, tombstones, standing like persons
in this enclosure closed in vain,
this tender air surrounding you
and this meadow all around you, happy,

don't they make you regret
at this moment, O indifferent stones,
your former fate when you were at least
a living corner of the living mountain?

What deadly lot links you with the dead
who, in spite of you, escape and mingle
with transformations, while you still
imitate their stiffness, horrible steles?

Ossuary

Are there only Victories
with broken wings?
And does love always let
embraced ones fall?

Who can recall the dead springs
and the smiles?
And this wave which carries us
moves toward the worst.

So that nothing will happen, we want
to stop ourselves.
But death is in a hurry, piling up
skull upon skull.

(Au Fond du Miroir le Double)

Au fond du miroir le double se confond
qu'on ne consulte davantage,
tandis que, dans son lit, le sombre moribond
aux souvenirs qui vaguement s'en vont,
en défaillant arrache son image.

Celui du miroir et lui qui meurt,
sont-ils tous deux d'accord à disparaître?
Ou, dans la glace, restera, peut-être,
un être à son tour provocateur?

(Tout Vous Dire)

Tout vous dire serait trop long.
D'ailleurs on lit dans la bible
en quoi le bon est nuisible,
en quoi le malheur est bon.

Invitons du nouveau
en unissant nos silences;
si, d'emblée, on avance,
nous le saurons tantôt.

Vers le soir pourtant il arrive
quand son souvenir s'entête,
qu'une curiosité tardive
devant la glace l'arrête.

On ne sait pas trop s'il a peur.
Mais il reste, il s'engage,
et devant sa propre image
se transporte ailleurs.

(The Double in the Mirror)

The double in the mirror is confused
because we don't consult him anymore,
while in his bed the sombre moribund
with memories that vaguely vanish,
tears off his image as he wastes away.

The mirrored and the dying one,
have they both agreed to disappear?
Or, perhaps, will there remain in the mirror
one who, in turn, is provocateur?

(Telling You All)

Telling you all would take too long.
Besides, we read in the Bible
how the good is harmful
and how misfortune is good.

Let's invite something new
by unifying our silences;
if, then and there, we advance,
we'll know it soon enough.

And yet toward evening,
when his memory is persistent,
one belated curiosity
stops him before the mirror.

We don't know if he is frightened.
But he stays, he is engrossed,
and, facing his reflection,
transports himself somewhere else.

(Reflet du Feu)

Peut-être n'était-ce qu'un reflet du feu
sur quelque meuble luisant
que beaucoup plus tard l'enfant
se rappelle comme un aveu.

Et si dans sa vie de plus tard
un jour, comme tant d'autres, le blesse,
c'est qu'il a pris comme promesse
un quelconque hasard.

N'oublions non plus la musique
qui tôt l'avait entraîné
vers l'absence que complique
une âme comblée. . . .

(Prisonniers)

Autrefois, qui chantait dans les tours?
Voix abandonnées des bouches blêmes. . . .
Sont-ce les mêmes
qui à présent se taisent aux carrefours?

Et ceux d'autrefois qui, ardemment,
sans but précis se perdaient sur les routes,
ont-ils pour héritiers ceux que le doute
retient à l'ombre de leur sang?

Au fond de nous, une liberté en deuil
envie la vôtre toujours en extase,
ô prisonniers des véritables tours;
et vous, les humbles pèlerins d'amour,
ce pas vers l'infini qui vous transvase,
n'était-il plein d'un éternel accueil?

(Fire's Reflection)

Perhaps it's no more than the fire's reflection
on some piece of gleaming furniture
that the child remembers so much later
like a revelation.

And if in his later life, one day
wounds him like so many others,
it's because he mistook some risk
or other for a promise.

Let's not forget the music, either,
that soon had hauled him
toward absence complicated
by an overflowing heart. . . .

(Prisoners)

Years ago, who sang in the towers?
Abandoned voices of pale mouths. . . .
Are they the same as those
now silent in the public squares?

And years ago those ardent ones
without specific goals who lost themselves en route,
are their descendants those whom doubt
now grips in the shadow of their blood?

At our depths, a mourning freedom
envies yours always in ecstasy,
O prisoners of genuine towers;
and you, love's humble pilgrims,
this step toward infinity now emptying you,
wasn't it filled with eternal welcome?

(L'Enfant devant la Glace)

L'enfant devant la glace s'étonne
et passe;
et personne ne ramasse
ce que son image lui donne.

(Les Morts)

Cœur de vieillard, qui dans sa morgue dort,
et d'autres qui renoncent et renient—
mais, ô combien qui dans leur crypte crient:
Encore! Encore!

Encore la peur, l'insulte, la tendresse
et l'angoisse qui nous plie—
tout ce qui charme et tout ce qui blesse—
enfin, tout ce qui fut la vie!

—Faisons du bruit, se disent ceux qui vivent,
entendre leurs regrets, à quoi bon?
—Ô mes amis, approchons de la rive,
et écoutons, et écoutons!

Il faut connaître la voix entière,
le son qui sort de nous n'est que le quart;
ces disparus nous parlent de la mère
à nous, les orphelins et les bâtards.

Ils nous demandent infiniment de vivre,
pour nous, pour ceux qu'on trompe, et pour eux;
le ciel résiste, mais la terre est ivre
de tant de bouches et de tous les yeux.

Ne croyez que fleurs et fruits consument
les innombrables morts inassouvis,

(The Child at the Mirror)

The child at the mirror
surprises himself and moves on;
and no one ever knows
what his reflection offers him.

(The Dead)

An old man's heart sleeping in its morgue
and others who renounce and deny—
but, oh, how many in their crypt cry out:
More! More!

More fear, insult, tenderness,
and anguish that doubles us over—
all that charms and all that wounds—
in short, all that was life!

—Let's make noise, the living say,
what good is hearing their regrets?
—O my friends, let's approach the shore
and listen, let's listen!

We must know the entire voice,
our sound is but a fourth;
to us, the orphans and the bastards,
the vanished speak about the mother.

They forever demand that we live
for ourselves, for those we wrong, and for them;
the sky resists, but the earth is drunk
with so many mouths and all those eyes.

Don't believe that fruits and flowers
consume the numberless unsatisfied dead,

autour de nous, il reste d'amertume
et de douceur un flottant infini.

Obéissons, non à la jouissance
qui tôt s'évanouit et prend trop peu—
mais aux murmures, mais aux influences,
mais à cet Ange vigoureux

qui entre nous, debout, et ceux qui gisent,
rapporte des messages et des cris,
pour qu'il attache à la terre promise
tous les élans de notre cœur promis!

Le Magicien

Le magicien, les yeux tout creux et vides,
émet le mot qui correspond. . . .
Et déjà naît, dans le silence aride,
le trouble sourd d'un gros remous fécond.

L'excite-t-il, ou bien déjà l'arrête?
Et qui l'emporte—est-ce le magicien?
On conçoit qu'un fait fatal complète
son geste qui ordonne et retient.

Le mot agit, et nul ne le reprend.
Soudain, à certaines heures, ce qu'on nomme
devient . . . quoi? Un être . . . presque homme,
et on le tue, en le nommant!

of bitterness and sweetness there remains
a floating infinity around us.

Let us obey, not that delight
vanishing too soon and taking too little—
but those murmurs, but those influences,
but this vigorous Angel

who, standing between us and those who stir,
brings back messages and cries
so that it may attach to the promised land
all the yearnings of our promised heart!

The Magician

His eyes shallow and empty, the magician
utters the corresponding word. . . .
And in the arid silence, the deaf chaos
of a great fertile tide is already born.

Does he excite it or already stop it?
And who carries it off—the magician?
We conceive just one complete fatal fact
that his gesture ordains and retains.

The word moves and no one captures it.
Suddenly, at certain hours, what we name
becomes . . . what? A being . . . almost human,
and, naming it, we kill it!

(Nul Ne Parle d'Eux)

Nul ne parle d'eux, et pourtant
ils étaient de vivre avides;
ils étaient plus que le vent
qui de nous parfois décide. . . .

Ils étaient purs et charmants.

Qui, dans les cimetières,
devine leurs noms effacés?
Ces simples noms de naguère
qu'ils avaient préférés

comme une fleur qu'on préfère.

Nous aimons tant du nouveau.
Ils étaient, ces jouvenceaux,
plus neufs certainement qu'il ne faut
pour étonner un tombeau.

Chanson Cruelle

Mettez-vous au saule,
là, au bout du pré;
contre votre épaule
vous le sentirez.

Prenez la cornemuse,
essayez un peu,
si la musique intruse
peut-être nous émeut.

Tant qu'elle nous commande
bien, nous danserons
parmi la lavande,
lui, le forgeron,

(No One Speaks of Them)

No one speaks of them, and yet
they were avid to live;
they were more than the wind
which sometimes decides our fate. . . .

They were charming and pure.

Who can guess their names
erased in cemeteries?
Those simple names of yesteryear
that they preferred

like a flower we prefer.

We love the new so much.
These striplings, certainly,
were newer than need be
to shatter a tomb.

Cruel Song

Stand by the willow,
there, at the meadow's
edge; you'll feel it rub
against your shoulder.

Pick up the bagpipe,
try it out a little,
see if that intrusive
music might move us.

As long as it commands
us well, we'll dance
among the lavender,
he, the blacksmith,

et moi, la bergère. . . .
Ne soufflez pas mot.
Si ça vous désespère,
vous pleurerez tantôt!

L'Orphelin

Je cours le long des routes, je cours,
j'ai le cœur affolé;
mon meilleur jour, ce sera le jour
où quelqu'un me dira: assez!

Et penser que c'est pour tout de bon!
Et dire que c'est la vie!
Je l'interroge, elle répond:
Nenni!

Les autres ont toujours leur espoir
qui se détache un peu.
Moi, ça fait du noir sur noir,
ou bien du noir sur du bleu.

(La Leçon)

Si j'avais assez su
de toutes les choses,
ton amour assidu
et qui m'impose,

m'eût donné beaucoup d'enfants.
J'aurais aimé à les entendre bruire
autour de moi, et de les instruire
m'eût été charmant.

and I, the shepherdess. . . .
Don't breathe a word.
If that makes you despair,
you can weep a little later!

The Orphan

I run along the road, I run,
my heart in a panic;
my best day will be the day
when someone says: enough!

And think that it's for good!
And say that it is Life!
I question her, she answers:
Ninny!

Others always have their hope
that stands out a little.
But for me it's black on black,
or a bit of black on blue.

(The Lesson)

If I'd known enough
about everything,
your diligent love
commanding my attention

would have given me many children.
I would have loved hearing them whisper
around me, and teaching them
would have been enchanting.

Mais il faut que moi-même j'apprenne
les moyens d'obéir;
un jour, quand il faudra finir,
j'aurai commencé à peine.

Départ

Mon amie, il faut que je parte.
Voulez-vous voir
l'endroit sur la carte?
C'est un point noir.

En moi, si la chose
bien me réussit,
ce sera un point rose
dans un vert pays.

Moment entre les Masques

On était déguisé, pendant qu'on restait dans
les chambres enfermé et dans les manteaux raides;
mais vers la fin d'hiver le carnaval nous aide
à *jouer* un instant au déguisement.

Car bientôt le printemps enlève tous les masques:
il veut un pays clair, un jardin franc;
déjà un air tout nu se penche sur la vasque
où l'eau attend les ombres du printemps.

Nous sentirons son corps s'étirer plein de sève,
mais sa figure, l'a-t-on jamais vue?
A peine adulte, il ne quitte plus
son masque de verdure qu'il achève.

But I myself must learn
the ways we must obey;
one day, when it is time to stop,
I will have just begun.

Departure

My friend, I have to go.
Do you want to see
the place on the map?
It is a black dot.

But if this turns out
well, then in me
it will be a spot of rose
in a green country.

Moment between Masks

As long as we stayed in closed rooms
and stiff coats, we were disguised;
but toward the end of winter the carnival
helps us to *play* at disguise for a while.

For soon spring will remove all the masks:
it wants a clear country, an honest garden;
already a fully naked air leans on the basin
where water waits for the shadows of spring.

We'll feel its body, full of sap, stretch,
but have we ever seen its face?
Barely adult, it never takes off
the mask of greenery it completes.

(Les Morts Lourds)

Nous nous portons; mais le poids des morts
s'ajoute-t-il à cette terre pour
l'arrêter net? Elle se meut encore,
malgré les morts qui tant nous semblent lourds.

Une fois en elle, ils ne pèsent plus
ces morts si lourds; c'est comme un livre lu
dont elle sait le contenu,
la terre lourde qui se meut toujours.

(Printemps)

Recommençons, dit la terre, recommençons,
c'est ma seule chance.
Et tout à coup le printemps s'écrie: On
recommence!

Et l'activité partout et l'action,
quelle obéissance.
Et le cœur qu'on voudrait retenir, d'un bond
se relance.

Seulement la terre qui obéit,
sait bien qu'elle tourne en rond,
tandis que nous vers l'infini
nous précipitons.

Enfant en Rouge

Parfois elle traverse le village dans sa petite robe rouge,
toute absorbée à se contenir,
mais, malgré elle, on dirait qu'elle bouge
selon un rythme de sa vie à venir.

(The Heavy Dead)

We move on; but does the weight
of the dead add itself to the Earth
to stop her cold? She is still moving,
despite the seemingly heavy dead.

Once inside of her, those heavy dead
no longer weigh; like a book she's read
and whose contents she already knows,
the always moving heavy Earth.

(Springtime)

Let's start again, says the Earth, start again,
it's my only chance.
And suddenly springtime cries out:
We're starting up again!

And everywhere action and activity,
such obedience.
And the heart we'd want to restrain starts
up again with one leap.

But the obedient Earth well knows
that she moves round and round,
whereas we hurtle down
toward infinity.

Child in Red

Sometimes she walks through the village in her little red dress,
all absorbed in restraining herself,
and yet, despite herself, she seems to move
according to the rhythm of her life to come.

Elle court un peu, hésite, s'arrête,
fait demi-tour...
et tout en rêvant secoue sa tête
contre ou pour.

Puis elle fait quelques pas d'une danse
qu'elle ébauche et oublie,
trouvant sans doute que la vie
trop vite avance.

Ce n'est pas tant qu'elle sorte
de son petit corps qui l'enferme,
mais tout ce qu'en elle elle porte
joue et germe....

C'est de cette robe qu'elle va se rappeler plus tard
dans un doux abandon;
quand toute sa vie sera pleine de hasards,
la petite robe rouge aura toujours raison.

(Lys Blanc)

Lys blanc, à force d'être tant
blanc—que devenir?
Il rêve, en reflétant
de toutes les couleurs un soupir.

Autour de lui, le jardin
jette un éclat éperdu;
son blanc, dans l'ombre, est plein
de tant d'absences émues....

She runs a bit, hesitates, stops,
half-turns around . . .
and, all while dreaming, shakes her head
for or against.

Then she dances a few steps
that she invents and forgets,
no doubt finding out that life
moves on too fast.

It's not so much that she steps out
of the small body enclosing her,
but that all she carries in herself
frolics and ferments.

It's this dress that she'll remember
later in a sweet surrender;
when her whole life is full of risks,
the little red dress will always seem right.

(White Lily)

White lily, just by dint of being
so white—to come to what?
While reflecting a sigh
from all other colors, it dreams.

The garden scatters a desperate
brilliance around it;
in shade, its white is full
of so many stirring absences. . . .

(Les Vierges Sages et Folles)

Je les vois comme une ancienne estampe,
tiges sveltes et belles corolles:
les vierges sages, les vierges folles
avec leurs lampes.

Les unes défaites, les autres prospères;
mais celles qui tiennent l'intacte lumière,
ne souffrent-elles guère,
douces esclaves,
de l'inutile forme suave
qu'elle éclaire?

Tandis que les autres, par maladresse,
les filles sombres,
douces esclaves,
reçoivent,
obéissantes,
les lentes caresses des ombres. . . .

Les Jouets

Ils ont bu et toujours rebu
notre plus vert amour;
mais au lieu d'être émues,
ces choses voulues
en bois, en papier, en velours,
boudent. . . .

On leur a donné
tendresse et charité,
pour les défendre. . . .
Mais si on voulait reprendre
un peu de cette identité:
elles sont des boîtes fermées
à clef.

(The Wise and Foolish Virgins)

I see them as an ancient print,
slender stems and lovely corollas:
the wise virgins, the foolish virgins
with their lamps.

These are wasted, the others prosper;
but those who keep the light intact,
don't they suffer a little,
those soft slaves,
from the soft useless shape
they light up?

While the others, by mistake,
the sombre girls,
those soft slaves,
receive,
obediently,
the slow caress of shadows. . . .

Toys

They have drunk and always re-drunk
our greenest love;
but instead of being moved,
these wished-for things
of wood, of paper, of velour,
sulk. . . .

We gave them
tenderness and charity
to protect them. . . .
But if we want to take back
a bit of that identity:
they are boxes
locked with keys.

Comme un voleur on voudrait
dans la nuit épaisse
forcer ces jouets
et se venger de leur paresse,
de leur indécence béate.
Mais comment trouver
dans leur graisse de ouate
un peu de chaleur perdue...?

On les renie, on part....
Mais d'autres enfants
à leur temps,
en mal de prélude,
restent pensifs et hagards
devant tant d'ingratitude.

Chanson

Jouons aux bergers, et que tes charmes
soient les brebis de mon troupeau
qui, peureux et doux, à toute alarme
de mon cœur accourent aussitôt.

Gentiment tu portes à sa bride
ton chapeau en panier pastoral;
tout est juste, rien ne m'intimide,
et mon cœur ne bat pas mal.

C'est le temps de verser dans ma flûte
tout mon souffle qui se préparait,
car l'ancienne prude que vous fûtes
part avec la brute que j'étais.

Notre jeu me semble tout à nous.
Et les loups de notre bergerie
ne sont là que parce qu'à la vie
d'un si beau berger il faut des loups.

Like a thief
in thick night, we want
to pry these toys open
and avenge their laziness,
their smug indecency.
But how can we find
a little lost warmth
in their cotton-batting fat...?

We renounce them, we leave....
But other children
in their own time,
in a prelude of pain,
remain pensive and drawn
before so much ingratitude.

Song

Let's pretend we are shepherds,
your charms the sheep in my flock who,
fearful and mild, at every scare
quickly run back to my heart.

You gracefully carry your bonnet
by its ribbons, like a country basket;
all is well, nothing frightens me,
and my heart isn't beating hard.

It's time to pour into my flute all
my breath that's been preparing itself,
for the old-fashioned prude that you were
is leaving with the brute that I was.

Our play seems entirely our own.
And the wolves in our sheep-pen
are there only because in such a handsome
shepherd's life there must be wolves.

Le Masque

À Hermann Haller

Ce matin, en entrant dans ma chambre,
j'avais oublié ta présence:
masque de femme orientale
fait par un grand sculpteur.
Frayeur sacrée de trouver là
où on se croit seul
plus que figure.
Et de sentir que la mienne
te contemplant,
face comblée,
ne saurait t'égaler.

(Nostalgie)

Ô ma vie, que je voudrais être celui qui répond
à ton plus juste désir. Ô ma vie,
en te voyant, plus tard, dira-t-on
que mon ardeur n'a point suffi
à te remplir tout entière, ma vie—
que dis-je, à t'exalter,
à trouver le secret qui multiplie
tes possibilités?
Enfin, à te découvrir, ma vie,
là où tout germe encore,
dans cette terre qui unifie
la vie et la mort.
Dans ta terre intime, ma vie,
d'où fut tiré mon cœur,
et dont le ciel n'est que nostalgie
de la terrestre splendeur.

The Mask

For Hermann Haller

Entering my room this morning,
I had forgotten your presence:
mask of an oriental woman
carved by a great sculptor.
Sacred terror of finding there,
where we think we are alone,
more than a face.
And of feeling that my own,
contemplating you,
total face,
could not equal you.

(Nostalgia)

O my life, how I'd want to be he who responds
to your most exact desire. Seeing you
later on, O my life, will it be said
that my ardor did not suffice
to fill you completely, my life—
what can I say to exalt you,
to find the secret that multiplies
your possibilities?
To discover you at last, my life,
there where all is germinating still,
in this earth that unifies
life and death.
In your intimate earth, my life,
from whence my heart was drawn
and whose sky is just nostalgia
for terrestrial splendor.

(Calme des Animaux)

Calme des animaux dont l'inquiétude
ne jamais insiste
(comme elle fait chez nous) à les rendre tristes
par habitude.

Qu'est-ce qu'ils savent, eux, quel bonheur qu'on nous cache
les remplit de cette prudente mesure?
Et pourtant, eux aussi, l'amour les arrache
à eux-mêmes et les torture.

La vie n'est pas tendre pour eux; sans être ingrate,
elle est rude souvent, à force d'être forte.
Même la plus tendre vie se comporte
selon la couleur de ce sang écarlate.

Cependant, ce sont eux qui ne dorment jamais en vain,
car leur sommeil comme des cailloux les roule;
ils en ressortent, refondus dans son moule
et leur neuve envie rend tout neuf le matin.

Ils ignorent.... Est-ce cela? Ils ignorent
cette science et demie dont nous savons un quart;
ils se remplissent de vie comme la calme amphore
et leur interne loi comprend le hasard.

Tout est juste pour eux, même telle injustice
qui les fait souffrir et plier.
C'est leur cœur innocent qui contient cette heure propice
qu'aucun sort ne saurait renier.

(The Calm of Animals)

The calm of animals for whom anxiety
never insists
(as it does in us) on making them
habitually unhappy.

What do they know, what joy hidden from us
fills them with this prudent measure?
And yet, love tears them out
of themselves, too, and tortures them.

Life is not tender toward them; though not unproductive,
it is often rough because it is so strong.
Even the tenderest life behaves
according to the color of this scarlet blood.

Meanwhile, they are the ones who never sleep in vain,
for their sleep rolls them like pebbles;
they come out of it again, recast in its mold,
and their new longing makes the morning wholly new.

They ignore. . . . Is that it? They ignore
this science-and-a-half about which we know but a fourth;
they fill themselves again with life like a calm amphora
and their internal law fully knows the danger.

All is just for them, even the very injustice
that makes them suffer and break.
But their innocent hearts contain this propitious hour
that no fate will know how to deny.

(Seins)

Quelle chance de porter deux petits seins
vers quelqu'un, vers l'inconnu. . . .
Deux petits seins qui disent: peut-être demain . . .
et qui, sans rien de plus,
sont heureux. Entre eux le médaillon
avec la douce image de la mère repose;
on dirait que sa protection
les sépare, ces deux seins, pour que la jeune fille n'ose
les sentir tous les deux à la fois,
ces petits seins juvéniles que l'on doit
porter à quelqu'un, à l'inconnu,
et qui vivent un peu à l'insu
de la porteuse.
Vont-ils la rendre heureuse,
ces deux petits seins innocents
qui résistent aux vents
de la vie? Ces petits seins têtus,
d'un semblant de deuil revêtus
contre lequel ils posent,
sous d'imperceptibles alertes,
leurs tendres demandes de roses
couvertes.

L'Enfant

Avoir encore les plantes des pieds à peu près neuves
et l'œil à peine rusé,
et pouvoir demander à ce corps peu usé
les innombrables preuves
de son envie d'avenir.
Comment ne pas sentir
entre les neuves paupières
les clartés auxiliaires
de ce clair émail beau

(Breasts)

How fortunate to bear two small breasts
toward someone, toward the unknown. . . .
Two small breasts that say: perhaps tomorrow . . .
and which, with nothing more,
are happy. The locket with the sweet
picture of the mother rests between them;
it's as if its protection
separates these two breasts so the young girl
won't dare feel both of them at once,
these small adolescent breasts that must be
borne toward someone, toward the unknown,
and which exist a little without
the bearer's knowledge.
Will they make her happy,
these two small, innocent breasts
which resist the winds
of life? These small stubborn breasts
seemingly dressed in mourning,
against which, under
imperceptible alerts, they pose
their tender demands like covered
roses.

The Child

To still have footholds that are almost new
and a barely cunning eye,
and to be able to demand from this barely used body
the innumerable proofs
of its longing for the future.
How can we not feel,
between these new eyelids,
the auxiliary gleams
of this lovely bright glaze

qui semble sortir des mains d'un orfèvre?
Ou cet imperceptible bord où la peau
s'amincit, transparente, pour devenir lèvre?
Et cet espace inédit entre les doigts qui s'écartent,
laissant tout écouler comme sable et eau....
Et ces mots, montrés comme un jeu de cartes,
où l'on gagne trop tôt.

(Grain Ailé)

Salut! Grain ailé qui s'envole vers
son sort, à gauche, à droite....
Que ton vol doit être cher
aux hasards qui te convoitent.

Ils se croient puissants, chacun d'eux,
par son souffle perfide;
mais à la fin tu hésites un peu....
C'est ton hésitation qui décide.

(Choses Perdues)

Vous souvient-il de ces choses que l'on a perdues le lendemain?
Une dernière fois elles vous implorent
(en vain)
de rester auprès de vous encore.

Mais l'ange des pertes les a frôlées de son aile distraite;
on ne les tient plus, on les arrête.

Elles ont reçu, sans que nous sachions quand,
les stigmates d'absence;
malgré les fenêtres fermées, un vent
subtil vers elles s'avance.
Elles vont sortir de cet ordre précis

that seems to spring from a goldsmith's hands?
Or this imperceptible edge where flesh,
transparent, thins to become lip?
And this original space between spreading fingers,
letting all flow through like sand and water. . . .
And these words, revealed like a game of cards
in which we win too soon.

(Winged Seed)

Hello! Winged seed flying
left and right toward your fate. . . .
How your flight must be dear
to the risks that covet you.

Each of them thinks it is strong
because of its treacherous breath;
but in the end you hesitate a bit. . . .
It's your hesitation that decides.

(Lost Things)

Do you remember things you've lost, the next day?
For one last time they implore you
(in vain)
to still stay next to you.

But the angel of losses has brushed them with his distracted wing;
we no longer hold them, we stop them.

Without our knowing when, they have received
the stigmatas of absence;
despite the closed windows, a subtle wind
advances toward them.
They will step out of this precise order

de la possession qui les nomme.
Bientôt, quelle sera leur vie
qui ne sera plus la vie de l'homme
qui les avait aimées? Auraient-elles aussi
de longs regrets parmi les poussières moroses?
Ou est-ce que les choses
s'entreaident vers un oubli
plus prompt? Le vague bonheur d'être matière
les reprend-il, les rendant à l'aveugle mère
qui les touche et leur reproche à peine
d'avoir subi la pensée humaine?

(Jugements)

Si c'est un Dieu qui nous défait: obéissons!
Il saura recréer: qu'il nous détruise.
Mais, ô terrible sort que d'être aux prises
avec nos propres mains qui nous défont

irrémédiablement et de la sorte
que rien de nous ne pourra ressusciter;
car cet avant-dernier jugement l'emporte,
bien autrement cruel, sur le dernier.

(Marteau d'Automne)

Déjà par ci et par là dans les prés,
un petit arbre s'allume;
morceau d'été
incandescent
que l'automne met sur l'enclume,
frappé par le marteau du temps.

of possession that names them.
Soon, what will be their life
that won't be the life of the person
who had loved them? Will they also have
long regrets among the gloomy dusts?
Toward what faster oblivion
are things helping
one another? Does the vague joy of being matter
seize them again, returning them to the blind mother
who touches and hardly reproaches them
for having suffered human thought?

(Judgments)

If it's a God who tears us down, let us obey!
He knows how to recreate: let him destroy us.
But, O the terrible fate to be in the grip
of our own hands which can destroy us

irreparably and in such a way
that nothing of us could resurrect;
for this next-to-final judgment, so cruel
otherwise, carries it up to the last.

(Autumn Hammer)

Already, here and there in the meadow,
a small tree catches fire;
incandescent
piece of summer
autumn places on the anvil
struck by time's hammer.

Marteau, ô marteau,
qui de si haut
revient,
forges-tu un tombeau,
grand marteau aérien?

Ou, nous frappant aussi
(métal qui retentit
sous tant de coups),
voudrais-tu faire de nous,
marteau, marteau,
l'urne d'airain debout
sur ce tombeau?

(Papillon)

L'ombre d'un papillon.
Est-ce qu'un dieu considère
son apparition éphémère
comme nous considérons
celle qui nous est chère?

(Bonheur Blanc)

Celle qui n'est pas venue, n'était-elle quand même
forte à organiser et à orner mon cœur?
S'il fallait exister pour être celle qu'on aime,
en quoi un cœur serait-il créateur?

Beau bonheur laissé en blanc, tu es peut-être le centre
de tous mes labeurs et amours.
Si je t'ai tant pleuré, c'est que je t'ai préféré entre
tant de bonheurs à contours.

Hammer, O hammer,
returning
from so high,
are you forging a tomb,
huge aerial hammer?

Or, also striking us
(metal that rings
under so many blows),
would you make of us,
hammer, hammer,
the brass urn standing
on this tomb?

(Butterfly)

The shadow of a butterfly.
Does some god consider
its apparition ephemeral,
just as we consider
someone who is so dear to us?

(Blank Joy)

She who did not come, wasn't she determined
nonetheless to organize and decorate my heart?
If we had to exist to become the one we love,
what would the heart have to create?

Lovely joy left blank, perhaps you are
the center of all my labors and my loves.
If I've wept for you so much, it's because
I preferred you among so many outlined joys.

(Dans la Vie d'Oubli)

Y a-t-il peu dans la vie de cet oubli que désirent
ceux qui n'ont jamais compris
combien tout se soutient, se répond et s'attire
dans un échange infini?

Moi, au contraire, depuis mon enfance j'admire
comme dans ce monde ouvert
aucun regard supporté, aucun sourire,
nulle douceur ne se perd.

Tout nous revient. Chaque cœur, si on ne l'arrête,
selon son rythme inné,
ferait tout le parcours, la douce ronde complète
de sa secrète fidélité.

Narcisse

Entourée de son bras comme d'un coquillage,
elle entend son être qui murmure,
tandis que lui supporte cet outrage
de son image à jamais trop pure. . . .

Pensivement en suivant leur exemple,
en elle-même rentre la nature:
la fleur qui dans sa sève se contemple
s'attendrit trop, et le rocher s'endure. . . .

C'est le retour de tout désir qui rentre
vers toute vie qui de loin s'enlace. . . .
Où tombe-t-il? Veut-il, sous la surface
qui dépérit, renouveler un centre?

(In This Life of Neglect)

In this life of neglect, is there anything desired
by those who have never understood
how all things support, answer, and attract each other
in an infinite exchange?

Since childhood, however, I have admired
how, in this open world,
no sustained glance, no smile,
not one tenderness is lost.

All comes back to us. If it isn't stopped, each heart,
according to its own rhythm,
will run the whole course, the complete tender round,
of its secret fidelity.

Narcissus

Encircled by her arms as by a shell,
she hears her being murmur,
while forever he endures
the outrage of his too pure image. . . .

Wistfully following their example,
nature re-enters herself:
contemplating its own sap, the flower
becomes too soft, and the boulder hardens. . . .

It's the return of all desire that enters
toward all life embracing itself from afar. . . .
Where does it fall? Under the dwindling
surface, does it hope to renew a center?

(Des Masques Se Tendent)

Des masques se tendent à nous,
mais on sent en dessous
les visages qui se plissent
et qui, sous prétexte d'abandon,
intimement satisfont
à leur goût d'avarice.

Tout est double; à tout
une grâce suppositive
prête ce trouble remous
entre deux rives.

L'Avenir

L'avenir: cette excuse du temps
de nous faire peur;
projet trop vaste, morceau trop grand
pour la bouche du cœur.

Qui t'aura jamais attendu, avenir?
Tout le monde s'en va.
Il te suffit d'approfondir
l'absence que l'on a.

Maternité

Ma vie, tu me l'as remplie
de ton parfum d'absence,
mon fils dans l'infini,
ô ma substance!

Toujours à genoux vers toi
lentement je m'avance.

(Masks Offer Themselves)

Masks offer themselves to us,
but beneath them we feel
faces that pucker
and, feigning surrender,
intimately satisfy
their taste for avarice.

All is double; an assumed
grace lends to all
this turbulent trouble
between two shores.

The Future

The future: time's excuse
to frighten us; too vast
a project, too large a morsel
for the heart's mouth.

Future, who won't wait for you?
Everyone is going there.
It suffices you to deepen
the absence that we are.

Motherhood

You refilled my life
with your perfume of absence,
my son in infinity,
O my substance!

Always kneeling toward you,
I move forward slowly.

J'ai les genoux si froids
depuis ta partance.

Dans mon trop vaste regard
rien ne plus compte.
Peut-on partir si tôt! J'ai honte
d'être si tard.

Saint-Sulpice

Tout s'accorde parfaitement
avec cette ombre dévalant
de l'église haute;
ce fleuriste effacé
et l'étalage à côté
de la pâtisserie dévote.

Cet étalage pacifié,
plein d'innombrables objets pieux
entre Madeleine et Pacôme,
et le patron de ce même lieu
qui s'appelle Percepied
pour ne pas s'appeler Perce-paume.

La Danse dans l'Escalier

Ce Monsieur du premier
qui dans le mur s'enfonce
est tout prêt de renier
sa demeure: il renonce.

Je n'habite plus nulle part
et votre passage blâme
même ce désir, Madame,
de loger dans votre regard.

My knees have been so cold
since your departure.

In my too vast concern
nothing matters more.
We're leaving? So soon!
I'm ashamed to be so late.

Saint Sulpice

All is in perfect harmony
with this shadow tumbling
from the lofty church;
the faded flower shop
and, next door, the simple
bakery's display.

Then this peaceful display,
full of countless pious objects,
between Madeleine and Pacôme,
and the owner of this place
who calls himself Lightfoot
so he won't be called Light-Fingered.

The Dance on the Staircase

The gentleman from the second
floor who sinks into the wall
is very close to giving up
his quarters: he gives up.

I now have no place to live,
and your passage, Madame,
even censures this desire
to lodge in your glance.

Chanson

Toi, à qui je ne confie pas
mes longues nuits sans repos.
Toi qui me rends si tendrement las,
me berçant comme un berceau.
Toi qui me caches tes insomnies,
dis, si nous supportions
cette soif qui nous magnifie,
sans abandon?

Car rappelle-toi les amants,
comme le mensonge les surprend
à l'heure des confessions.

Toi seule, tu fais partie de ma solitude pure.
Tu te transformes en tout: tu es ce murmure
ou ce parfum aérien.
Entre mes bras: quel abîme qui s'abreuve de pertes.
Ils ne t'ont point retenue, et c'est grâce à cela, certes,
qu'à jamais je te tiens.

Le Christ Ressuscité

Comment rester avec ce corps, comme un grain
blessé afin qu'il repousse,
dans ce tertre d'impatience tout plein
sous la printanière secousse?

Comment isoler ce cœur végétal
de l'environnante Nature
qui professe que nul n'arrête le mal
à moins qu'il le transfigure?

Song

You, to whom I don't confide
my long nights without rest.
You, who makes me so tenderly tired,
rocking me like a cradle.
You, who hides your insomnias from me,
tell me if, without surrender,
we will endure
this thirst that magnifies us?

For remind yourself of lovers,
how the lie surprises them
when the time comes to confess.

Only you are part of my pure solitude.
You transform yourself into all: you are this whisper
or this heavenly perfume.
Between my arms: such an abyss priming itself with losses.
They did not hold you back, and it's thanks to that,
surely, that I hold you forever.

The Resurrected Christ

To make it grow again like a wounded
seed, how to remain with this body
in this hillock full of impatience
under the vernal moment?

How to isolate the vegetal heart
of surrounding Nature
professing that nothing stops evil
unless it transfigures it?

Le Grand Pardon

À Mademoiselle Adrienne Monnier

On raconte, mais est-ce qu'on sait?
Quelque part l'Ange de l'Oubli,
radieux, tend sa figure au vent
qui tourne nos pages. Borne pure.
Et derrière lui tout ce pays
que nul plus ne saurait apprendre:
qu'il faut avoir su, autrefois,
morceau par morceau, tel que nos sens,
tel que la colère nous le cassait
à nos besoins. (Sans vouloir à présent
nier les inattendues guérisons
entre les choses, qui nous prenaient à témoins
sans que nous eussions jamais su les appeler. . . .
Et malgré tout, les fruits
supportaient nos noms, et les astres
ne les secouaient que rarement:
ces noms spongieux qui buvaient des larmes. . . .
Ces noms dont le plus tendre encore
n'est que le moule d'un cri.)

Les «Victoires»

Aucune n'avait plus ses ailes tout entières,
et, cependant, parées d'un vent ancien et vif,
les voici: portant la preuve millénaire
de leur vol victorieux à nos corps évasifs.

Nous sommes bien leurs fils par nos élans intimes,
leurs frères, tard-venus, par notre vol brisé,
mais rien qu'en soulevant leurs statues maritimes
dorées d'un beau soleil, de la mer irisées,

(ces ex-votos laissés par des navigateurs
au seuil des temples que nul dévot n'inquiète),

The Great Pardon

For Mademoiselle Adrienne Monnier

We talk about it, but do we know?
Somewhere the Angel of Oblivion,
radiant, offers his shape to the wind
that turns our pages. Pure boundary.
And behind him that whole country
no one else will know how to learn:
which, before, had to be learned
piece by piece, just as our feelings,
just as passion broke it for us
as we needed it. (Now, without wanting
to deny the unexpected healings
between things that called us to witness
without our ever knowing what to call them. . . .
And in spite of all, the fruits
endured our names, and the stars
rarely shook them off:
those spongy names that drank up tears. . . .
Those names among which the most tender
is still only the cast of a cry.)

The "Victories"

None still had their entire wings,
and yet, trimmed by an ancient and brisk wind,
here they are: bearing the millennial proof
of their victorious flight to our evasive bodies.

Surely, in our most secret leaps, we are their sons,
their late-coming brothers in our broken flight,
but just by raising their seafaring statues
gilded by a lovely sun, the iridescence of the sea,

(these ex-votos left by navigators
on the sill of temples no devotee cares about),

rien qu'en les soulevant au-dessus de nos têtes,
on est d'un cœur plus haut, et plus grand d'une sœur.

(Nos Pleurs)

Les Anges aiment nos pleurs,
de cette rosée avides;
parfois nous sommes des leurs
de par nos joues humides.

En partant ils sèchent d'un coup
d'aile notre figure,
sans jamais la voir si pure,
déjà loin de nous. . . .

L'Attente

C'est la vie au ralenti,
c'est le cœur à rebours,
c'est une espérance et demie:
trop et trop peu à son tour.

C'est le train qui s'arrête en plein
chemin sans nulle station,
et on entend le grillon
et on contemple en vain,

penché à la portière,
d'un vent que l'on sent, agités
les prés fleuris, les prés
que l'arrêt rend imaginaires.

just by raising them above our heads,
we are a heart taller and a sister greater.

(Our Tears)

Avid for that dew,
the Angels love our tears;
sometimes we are theirs
because of our humid cheeks.

Leaving, they dry our face
with the stroke of a wing,
never seeing it so pure,
already far from us. . . .

The Wait

It is life in slow motion,
it's the heart in reverse,
it's a hope-and-a-half:
too much and too little at once.

It's a train that suddenly
stops with no station around,
and we can hear the cricket,
and, leaning out the carriage

door, we vainly contemplate
a wind we feel that stirs
the blooming meadows, the meadows
made imaginary by this stop.

(Le Vent)

Je vois deux yeux comme deux enfants
errant dans une forêt.
Ils disent: qui nous mange c'est le vent, le vent—
et moi je reponds: je le sais.

Je connais une fille qui pleure, son amant
il-y-a deux ans s'en allait,
mais elle dit tout doucement: c'est le vent, le vent—
et moi je réponds: je le sais.

Souvent dans ma chambre en m'éveillant
il me semble qu'une langue me parlait.
Toi! Mais la nuit murmure: le vent—
et je pleure dans mon lit: je le sais.

(Ce Sont les Jours)

Ce sont les jours où les fontaines vides
mortes de faim retombent de l'automne,
et on devine de toutes les cloches qui sonnent
les lèvres faites des métaux timides.

Les capitales sont indifférentes.
Mais les soirs inattendus qui viennent
font dans le parc un crépuscule ardent,
et aux canaux avec les eaux si lentes
ils donnent une rêve vénitienne
et une solitude aux amants.

(The Wind)

I see two eyes like two children
wandering in a forest.
They say: what gnaws us is the wind, the wind—
and I reply: I know.

I know a girl who weeps, her lover
left two years ago,
but she says very softly: it's the wind, the wind—
and I reply: I know.

Often, as I awaken in my room,
it seems a tongue was talking to me.
You! But the night murmurs: the wind—
and in my bed I weep: I know.

(These Are the Days)

These are the days when empty fountains,
dead of starvation, collapse under autumn again,
and from all the ringing bells we can
detect the lips made of timid metals.

The capitals are indifferent.
But the unexpected nights that come
make a warm twilight in the park;
they give a Venetian dream
to the slow waters of canals
and privacy to lovers.

(Nuits Perdues)

Mes yeux, mes yeux sont las.
Je vois au fenêtre assise
un cheval, une mère, une brise
et les jours qui vont et passent.

Je vois le soir solennel.
Le soir des petites villages.
Il est clos comme une image
couleur d'or et grave comme le miel.

Et puis la nuit s'avance
et prend les places et les rues
et je pleure de mon enfance
et de toutes les nuits perdues.

Jour d'Été

La maison blanche, les persiennes closes,
s'est fermée comme une bouche après un cri;
sur le cadran le paon se repose
effaçant toutes les heures du midi.

On sent: ce soir s'effeuilleront les roses,
trop pleines d'elles-mêmes, en douces agonies.
Ô mon enfant, ô mon amie vas y—
la vie s'éclaire dans la mort des choses.

(Lost Nights)

My eyes, my eyes are tired.
Sitting at the window, I see
a horse, a mother, a clearing
and the days that come and go.

I see the solemn evening.
The evening of small towns.
It is as closed as a golden
image and as grave as honey.

And then night comes
and overtakes places and roads,
and I weep for my childhood
and for all the nights I have lost.

Summer Day

Its shutters closed, the white house
closed itself like a mouth after a cry;
the peacock rests on the clock,
erasing all the hours of noon.

We feel: tonight roses, too full of themselves,
will shed their petals in soft agonies.
O my child, O my friend go—
life clarifies itself in the death of things.

(Automne)

L'automne sonne dans les feuilles vides,
   et ce qui chante
   c'est la pluie tombante
   dans les rides humides.

Tout s'éloigne, tout s'éteint, tout change,
même sur la route où nous nous trouvâmes.
Dans les allées
tout tristement se cherchent les anges
pour s'envoler
vers le midi des âmes. . . .

(Chanson Éloignée)

Ô chant éloigné, suprême lyre,
qui ne se donne qu'à celui qui ardemment
et sans repos supporte et endure
de son effort le long et doux martyre,
Ô chant qui naît le dernier pour conclure
l'enfance non terminée, le cœur d'antan.

Au fond de ce que je devrais encore
transformer en ardeur en sang en âme,
je sens (que vaguement mon doute réclame)
les mots massifs, les mots profonds en or.

(Fall)

Fall rings in the empty leaves,
    and the singing
    is the rain falling
    in the humid ridges.

All becomes far, all is extinguished, all changes,
even on the road where we found ourselves.
In the lanes
angels sadly search for one another
to fly away
to the high noon of souls. . . .

(Distant Song)

O distant song, supreme lyre,
giving itself only to him who, ardently
and without rest, bears and endures
the long, slow martyrdom of your strain,
O song born last in order to complete
the unended childhood, yesterday's heart.

At the core of what I must still
transform with ardor, blood, and soul,
I feel (what my doubt vaguely reclaims)
those massive words, those vast words of gold.

(Lieu Sacré)

J'admire immensément la force solitaire
bras en croix érigée tout en haut
et qui en oubliant de son calvaire
s'ouvre d'un geste beaux tel qu'un drapeau

au vent, au vent qui précédant l'aurore
élargit l'univers comme des poumons
et reçoit et reçoit encore
ses lointaines et ses environs

même quand advient la nuit qui les efface
de son sourire éternel;
ô lieu sacré, suprême place
où Dieu dépose les cœurs autour desquels

l'obscurité humaine s'illumine
de tous les sorts dont elle se sent emplie
afin que quelques-uns au moins devinent
l'attendrissement de l'infini.

(Sa Nuit d'Été)

Si je pourrais avec mes mains brûlantes
fondre ton corps autour ton cœur d'amante,
ah que la nuit deviendrait transparente
le prenant pour un astre attardé
qui toujours dès le premier temps des mondes
était perdu et qui commence sa ronde
et tâtonnant de sa lumière blonde
sa première nuit, sa nuit, sa nuit d'été.

(Sacred Place)

I admire the solitary power
of arms erected crosswise, high,
and which, by forgetting their calvary,
open in a handsome gesture like a flag

in the wind, the wind before dawn
enlarging the universe like lungs
and receiving, still receiving
its distant and surrounding places

even when night happens to come, erasing
them with its eternal smile;
O sacred place, supreme place
where God locates hearts around which

human darkness is enlightened
of all the fates it feels full of,
so that at least a few suspect
the mercy of the infinite.

(Its Summer Night)

If with my burning hands I could melt
the body around your lover's heart,
ah, how the night would be transparent,
mistaking it for a belated star
which from the first days of the world
was always lost and which begins its rounds
with its blonde light groping around to touch
its first night, its night, its summer night.

(Rien n'y Demeure)

J'ai bu toute la nuit le vin de l'amour, Bien-aimée, tel
    que l'étang toute la nuit boit la lune pleine.

Minuit passé l'Astre se jettait vers moi pour sauver son
    image qui se noyait.

Oh que le ciel est plein, Bien-aimée, de choses et d'images;
    mais au cœur, tout y était, rien n'y demeure.

(Dire une Fleur)

La terre comment fait-elle pour, en sa profondeur
terrible et tragique dont on a peur,
préparer la candeur d'une fleur heureuse?
Hélas, mon cœur est creux, ma main est creuse,
que naîtra-t-il jamais de mon malheur?

Ô terre terrienne, terre pleine de morts,
apprends-moi un peu de ton audace.
Et que je fasse
printemps pareil par un pareil effort
(car il faut vivre si on vit encore).

Ne suis-je de toi? Que ta vigueur
ne me méprise point, qui tout pénètre,
ma tête est triste mais j'ai le cœur champêtre;
il se pourrait bien que je dise une fleur.

(Nothing's Left)

All night I drank love's wine, Love,
    just as all night the pond drinks the full moon.

With moonlight gone, the planet shot toward me
    to rescue its drowning image.

O Love, the sky is full of things and images;
    but in the heart, where all once was, there is nothing left.

(To Speak a Flower)

In its terrible and tragic depth
that frightens us, how does the earth
prepare the candor of a happy flower?
Ah, my heart is empty, my hand is empty,
what shall ever come of my sorrow?

O earthly earth, earth full of dead,
teach me some of your audacity.
And, with the same effort,
let me make it to spring just the same
(for we must live if we are still alive).

Don't I come from you? Don't let your vigor,
penetrating me, mock me,
my head is sad but my heart is sound;
I might speak just one flower.

(De Père en Fils)

Refuse-toi à la vie complicable.
Regarde ta main près du pain sur la table:
comme c'est clair, ces deux choses sur la nappe claire,
de père en fils et de fils en père.

Aime de la terre la campagne céleste
et la joie, cachée par la peine manifeste,
la fenêtre tranquille et la porte sévère
de père en fils et de fils en père.

Et les choses à genoux toujours à leur place
et le chien qui remue et pourtant les surpasse,
très-doux croyant, ne doutant guère
de père en fils et de fils en père.

(Vent Orphelin)

Vent orphelin sur la place vide
tire un peu mon manteau.
Me dit-il: Sois mon guide?
Je veux bien. Vois-tu, les eaux,
les eaux toujours s'évadent
doucement comme les amants,
et retombent en ballade—
faisons autant, petit vent.

(From Father to Son)

Reject the complicated life.
Look at your hand near the bread on the table:
how clear those two things on the clear cloth are
from father to son and from son to father.

Love the earth's celestial countryside
and its joy, hidden by manifest pain,
the quiet window, the harsh door
from father to son and from son to father.

And those kneeling things always in place
and the dog who fidgets, yet outdoes them,
very gentle believer who hardly doubts
from father to son and from son to father.

(Orphan Wind)

In the empty square, an orphan wind
tugs a little at my coat.
Is it saying: Be my guide?
I do want to be. You see the waters,
the waters always evade themselves
softly like lovers,
and fall back again in song—
little wind, let us do much the same.

(Géranium)

À *Madame Helen Hessel*

Géranium qui éclate
au doux soir pluvieux,
que ta joie écarlate
me pénètre mieux

qu'un plus tendre présage.
Comme je suis convaincu
de ta rouge rage—
et le lent refus

de ce soir qui pleure
et qui murmure: assez—
je le connais: c'est l'heure
qui se dissout pour passer.

L'Offrande Fanée

Déesse à ta clémence de ce matin pâlie
il ne faut pas la fraîcheur provoquante
d'une rose d'aujourd'hui—et qu'elle soit lente
la main qui t'offre celle dont la vie
décline—non, qu'elle soit indifférente éblouie
admirons la pente—
du blanc qui souffre vers le blanc qui nie.

L'Enfant Maudit

Je pèse sur mon lit, maman, et tout ce que j'endosse
est comme brûlé le soir; je sais que cela t'étonne
ma veste qui s'en va quand tu la brosses
et la culotte d'hier qui n'est plus bonne.

(Geranium)

For Madame Helen Hessel

Geranium, exploding
in the soft rainy night,
how your scarlet joy
penetrates me more

than a more tender omen.
How I am convinced
by your red rage—
and by the slow refusal

of this night that weeps
and murmurs: enough—
I understand: it is time
dissolving itself to pass.

Faded Offering

Goddess, on this blanched morning your mercy
doesn't need the provocative freshness
of one of today's roses—and let the hand
that offers you one whose life is declining
be slow—no, let it be indifferent. Dazzled,
let us admire the gradient—
of white that suffers toward white that negates.

Cursed Child

Mother, I'm heavy on my bed, and everything I wear
seems to be burnt at night; I know that astounds you,
my vest vanishing when you brush it,
and yesterday's pants that aren't good anymore.

Et dis, pourquoi me faut-il tant de ruse
pour te sourire à toi qui n'est pas morte?
Mes yeux me semblent lourds: est-ce que j'use
la trame de la vie? Est-elle plus forte

autour des autres? Est-ce que je déchire
les jours trop minces par mon sang trop brusque?
Ferais-je mal aux pauvres choses jusque
dans mon sommeil qui en colère m'attire?

(Plaisir Amer)

Ô doux plaisir qui nous exalte vers
l'insuffisance du trop. Plaisir amer
d'où nous sortons retombant en nous-mêmes
comme une pluie d'été. Plaisir extrême
qui fut trop clair.

Fais au moins que la douleur créée
par ta gloire et notre ignorance
nous rende chère de la jeune absence
cette pureté immaculée.

(Survie)

De s'éveiller entre les bras de l'amie
qui après ma mort en elle,
me donne encore cette suprême survie
matinale qu'elle attend presque maternelle.

Je n'ai jamais rien eu qu'elle ne m'eût donné;
mon ardeur rétrospective
me fait croire que c'est elle qui crée
toute ma vie successive.

And tell me, why do I need so much guile
to smile at you who are not dead?
My eyes feel heavy: do I wear down
life's conspiracy? Is it stronger

around others? Do I tear
the too-thin days with my too-blunt blood?
Will I injure those poor things even
in my sleep, attracting me in anger?

(Bitter Pleasure)

O sweet pleasure lifting us toward
the indigence of excess. Bitter pleasure
which we leave as we fall back into ourselves
like summer rain. Ultimate pleasure
that was too clear.

See to it, at least, that the anguish
created by your glory and our ignorance,
beloved of new absence,
grants us this immaculate purity.

(Survival)

To awaken in the arms of a friend
who, after my death in her,
still offers me this supreme survival
of morning she attends like a mother.

I've had nothing she has not given me;
my retrospective ardor
convinces me that it was she
who created my whole life.

Quelle joie avais-je par moi-même ailleurs?
Je ne me rappelle qu'une:
des amandiers en fleurs que j'ai vus, tout en fleurs,
contre une terre brune. . . .

(*Victoire Qui Dors*)

Victoire qui dors sur tes ailes—
debout!
À la proue, à la proue
et que ta place te revèle
à nous,
petite Victoire.

Nous obéissons, mais en te voyant
on veut te boire.
Tu es la même dehors et dedans,
petite Victoire.

(*Verger*)

Mon beau verger que je sois l'adepte
de ton silence laborieux,
que mon oreille de toi accepte
l'imperceptible bruit que fait un Dieu,

en travaillant, divinement, à l'aise
dans son métier d'amour et de lenteur
où tout par une grâce japonnaise
devient ardent sans renier la fleur.

What joy did I have alone, before?
I can remember only one:
the almond tree in bloom, all in bloom,
against the brown earth. . . .

(Victory Asleep)

Asleep on your wings, Victory
stand up!
To the prow, to the prow,
and let your place reveal you
to us,
little Victory.

We obey, but seeing you
we want to drink you.
Little Victory,
you are the same inside and out.

(Orchard)

My lovely orchard, let me be
the expert of your laboring silence,
let my ear accept from you
the imperceptible noise a God makes

while working, divinely, at ease
in his loving, patient art where,
with a Japanese grace, all becomes
ardent without denying the flower.

(Balance)

Sur la balance de l'air
un rien que l'on ajoute
fait changer et trembler toute
la vie qui de nous se sert

pour se sentir elle-même.
(Si elle se sent tout fort
son plaisir extrême
nous fait penser à la mort.)

(Surprise des Anges)

Tout ce qui arrive
pose
un masque sur notre figure qui n'ose
jamais être définitive.

Ainsi nous passons pendant que la vie nous déguise.
Et cette figure étrange
dont personne ne s'avise,
sera-t-elle un jour la surprise
des Anges?

(Scale)

A nothing we add
on the scale of air
changes and troubles
all Life that uses us

so she can feel herself.
(If she feels strong,
her utmost pleasure
makes us think of death.)

(Angels' Surprise)

Everything that happens
places
a mask on our face that never dares
to be definitive.

Thus we live in life's disguise.
And will this strange face
no one revises
one day become the surprise
of Angels?

(Après-Midi d'une Inconnue)

C'est ton après-midi que j'ai vécue,
inconnue d'autrefois; il avait plu
mais vers le soir tu sortais, seule, pour
enfin là découvrir l'ancienne tour
que dès ton arrivée tu guettais de ta fenêtre,
ce passé en ruine et l'avenir
lorsque tu t'arrachais soudain
de cette chambre à l'hôtel des Bains
où l'heure lente paraissait languir
peut-être ne faisait qu'un. Ta montée vers ta vie
ô inconnue, d'un pas tout clandestin
combien ce chemin à chaque pas compris
semblait ton chemin. . . .

(Quelque Parfum)

Malgré le ciel encore bas
et cet air qui chancelle,
quelque chose nouvelle
flotte vers l'odorat.

Quelque parfum tout vert
discrètement se dégage.
Un plaisir déménage:
le printemps est ouvert.

(Unknown Woman's Afternoon)

It is your afternoon that I lived,
unknown woman of the past; it had rained,
but toward evening you went out alone—
to explore at last the ancient tower
which, since your arrival, you had watched
from your window (the past in ruins and the future)—
suddenly tearing yourself away
from that room at the Hôtel des Bains
where the slow hour seemed to languish so,
but perhaps no longer than one. Climbing toward your life
with such clandestine steps, O stranger,
how this road, with every step you took,
seemed to be your road. . . .

(Some Perfume)

Despite the sky that is still
slow and this faltering air,
something new begins
floating into odor.

Some perfume, entirely green,
frees itself discreetly.
A pleasure starts to move:
now springtime is open.

(L'Homme Entêté)

Cet homme est occupé d'un problème
auquel il revient comme une mouche:
toutes ces choses opposées, il voudrait qu'elles se touchent
quand même.

Il voudrait que ce Dieu qui les a faites
tout juste au milieu d'elles s'arrête—
cet homme qui infiniment s'entête,
c'est le poète.

(Heureux, Heureuse)

Qui les verra jamais, heureux, heureuse—
d'un franc accord se rendre au carrefour,
avant que la nécessité ne creuse
ces yeux de faim à l'imprudent amour?

Faut-il toujours répéter la souffrance
tant de fois soufferte jusqu'au bout?
Ô belles, à la première confidence,
arrêtez-nous!

(Pays Ardent)

Que cela me plaît de subir ton exemple,
pays ardent, pays laborieux
(presque partout on détruit les temples—),
toi, tu es si clair et si ample
comme la lente enfance d'un dieu.

(Stubborn Man)

This man is occupied by a problem
to which he returns like a fly:
he wants all opposing things
to touch each other just the same.

He wishes God who made them all
would stop right in the midst of them—
that man who is infinitely stubborn
is the poet.

(Happy Men and Women)

Who will ever see happy men and women
reach the square in open harmony
before necessity can hollow out
those famished eyes of heedless love?

Must we always repeat the suffering,
so often suffered, until the end?
O lovely women, with the primal secret,
make us stop!

(Ardent Country)

How pleased I am to submit to your example,
ardent country, hard-working country
(almost everywhere temples are being destroyed),
you, you are so clear and ample,
like the slow infancy of a god.

Comme l'enfance d'un dieu que l'on cache
chez des êtres durs et doués,
chaque chèvre et chaque vache
fait de son mieux pour ne pas l'avouer.

Mais il perce, mais il pénètre,
mais il ouvre des profondeurs. . . .
Et ce vent qui semble le maître
n'est que l'esclave de sa douceur.

(Consolez-Moi)

Consolez-moi où que vous êtes
étant seule on est vite à bout;
si je pose sur ce chemin ma tête,
qu'il me semble adouci par vous.

N'est-il pas possible qu'on se tende
même de loin un souffle doux,
et qu'un pur regret d'absence rende
un duvet à ces cailloux?

(Sommeil)

Peur de la table, peur de l'alcôve,
peur de l'effort qui demain m'attend—
ce qui me garde, ce qui me sauve
c'est le sommeil qui m'a vu enfant.

Il m'a connu, il doit me connaître,
à ceux qui sont simples, il reste bon;
lui, si profond: je ne suis qu'une fenêtre.
Il est la maison.

Like a god's infancy that we hide
among hard and gifted creatures,
every goat and every cow
does its best to ignore it.

But he pierces, but he penetrates,
but he opens the depths. . . .
And this wind that seems to be master
is but the slave of his tenderness.

(Comfort Me)

Comfort me from wherever you are—
alone, we are quickly worn out;
if I place my head on the road,
let it seem softened by you.

Could it be that even from afar
we offer each other a gentle breath,
and that a pure regret of absence
covers these stones with down?

(Sleep)

Afraid of the table, afraid of the alcove,
afraid of the effort that awaits me tomorrow—
what protects me, what saves me
is the sleep that saw me as a child.

It has known me, it must know me,
it continues being good to the simple;
it, so vast: I am but a window.
It is the house.

(Voici le Soir)

Voici le soir:
pendant tout un jour encore je vous ai beaucoup aimées,
collines émues.

C'est beau de voir.
Mais: de sentir à la doublure des paupières fermées
la douceur d'avoir vu. . . .

(Ombre)

Nuage qui se déplace
dans cet immense air lumineux
et qui étonne l'uni de ce bleu
par sa forme d'audace.

En plein soleil cette trêve
d'ombre atteint mon jardin: elle rend
pensifs les verts et les rouges. . . . Le blanc
se dérobe et rêve.

(Un Soir de Romance)

Des nuages décoratifs
composent un soir de romance;
un chemin s'en va évasif.
La neuve lune commence

un nouveau chapitre de nos
nuits . . . de ces nuits frêles
que l'on couche et qui se mêlent
à ces noirs horizontaux.

(Night Has Come)

Night has come:
for one whole day again I've loved you much,
stirring hills.

It's lovely, to see.
But: to feel in the lining of closed eyelids
the sweetness of having seen. . . .

(Shade)

Cloud that shifts
in this vast, luminous air
and astounds the blue's harmony
with its kind of audacity.

This shadow-truce reaches
my garden in full sunlight: it makes
the greens and reds pensive. . . . White
undresses and dreams.

(Evening Love Song)

Ornamental clouds
compose an evening love song;
a road leaves evasively.
The new moon begins

a new chapter of our nights . . .
of those frail nights
we stretch out and which mingle
with these black horizontals.

(Le Poète)

Le tendre poète s'appuie
au bord du jardin matinal,
l'antique nature remue
dans son bonheur intégral.

Est-ce le cœur du mythe
qui en lui maintenant se refait?
Bouche à deux doigts de la flûte—
mais le baiser était plus près.

(Gestes)

Si l'on me demande si je voulais être
de celle qui pourrait venir, l'amant,
il m'arriverait de répéter peut-être
le geste que ce saule fait au vent.

Consentement ou doux refus? Que sais-je.
C'est un des mouvements distraits et purs
dont la nature qui connaît la neige
s'excuse d'être faible à l'azur.

(The Poet)

The gentle poet pauses
near the morning garden,
ancient nature stirs
in her integral happiness.

Is it the heart of myth
that now remakes itself in him?
Mouth two fingers from the flute—
but the kiss was even closer.

(Gestures)

If asked if I would want to be
the lover of the woman who might come,
perhaps I'd manage to repeat
the willow's gesture in the wind.

Consent or gentle refusal? I don't know.
It's one of those pure, oblivious gestures
with which nature, who knows all about snow,
excuses herself for being weaker in azure.

Notre-Dame

1

Voûte traversée de divines réponses. . . .

2

Menacées par l'approche du calme divin,
les orgues se déchaînent.
Saura-t-on dompter à la fin
ces forces indigènes?

Au silence qui nous détruit
elles font un bruit complémentaire,
criant à la nuit-mère
de notre étrange nuit.

(Bruit d'un Cœur)

On se penche dehors
vers un vague ailleurs:
c'est ce monde encore
dont on meurt.

Être ce vent cette nuit,
comme cela reposerait
du silence, du bruit
qu'un cœur fait.

Notre Dame

1

Arch traversed by divine answers. . . .

2

Menaced by the coming of divine calm,
the organs break loose.
Will these native powers
finally be tamed?

They make a noise complementing
the silence that destroys us,
crying from our own strange
night to Mother-Night.

(Heart's Noise)

We lean outdoors toward
some vague elsewhere:
it is still the world
that we are dying of.

To be this wind tonight,
how that would restore
the silence, the noise
that one heart makes.

(Border un Enfant)

Border un enfant dans son lit,
fermer cette lettre de vie
qui arrivera ce soir.
On la lira en compagnie,
ce qu'elle contient sera dit
à haute voix dans le noir.

Ce qu'elle contient finira
par créer du changement;
on s'arrêtera, on ira,
la chambre entière chavirera
dans cet être dormant.

Croquis

Au bord du lac, dans l'air blond,
sous un saule qui dit à demain,
des canots en rouge repeints
comme des tranches de melons
s'offrent à la saison
qui a faim.

(Partons)

Partons, partons! Vois-tu, les nuages
laissent là-bas un arrière-plan ouvert:
sous des clartés de nacre, c'est la plage,
le bord d'argent d'un continent en fer.

Partons, élançons-nous vers la trouée,
un coup de cœur vaut bien un coup de tête;
et faisons la conquête
de l'étendue si rarement avouée.

(Tuck a Child)

Tuck a child in his bed,
close this letter of life
that will arrive tonight.
We will read it together,
its contents will be spoken
out loud in the dark.

What it contains will end
by creating changes;
we will stop, we will go,
the whole room will capsize
in this sleeping one.

Sketch

At the edge of the lake, in yellow light,
under the willow saying tomorrow,
small dinghies freshly painted red
like slices of melon
offer themselves
to the hungry season.

(Let's Leave)

Let's leave, let's leave! See, the clouds
leave an open background out there:
under bright mother-of-pearl is a beach,
the silver edge of an iron continent.

Let's leave, launch ourselves toward that breach,
a beat of the heart is worth a nod of the head;
and let us conquer
that expanse so rarely acknowledged.

(Lire les Fleurs)

On a lu les tulipes, on a lu
deux strophes de jonquilles:
distrait assez et très ému—
comme lisent les jeunes filles.

Les terrasses forment un sonnet
de leurs gradins qui reculent;
l'apparition d'un chardonneret
y pose une virgule.

Coucou

Depuis tant de semaines tout nous dispute nos
règles d'hiver. Il faudra, il faut
désarmer, s'adoucir, laisser faire
l'inévitable printemps héréditaire.

Déjà le nid dans mon oreille est assez doux
pour que ta voix y vienne, coucou.
Dépose dans cet écrin le long collier de tes cris
dont le fermoir perdu nous occupe. Tant pis!

(Reading Flowers)

We read the tulips, we read
two strophes of jonquils:
distracted enough and very moved—
the way that young girls read.

The terraces compose a sonnet
with their receding tiers;
the appearance of a goldfinch
adds a punctuation mark.

Cuckoo

For so many weeks now everything
disputes our winter rules. We should,
we must disarm, become more mild,
allow the inevitable hereditary spring.

The nest in my ear is soft enough already
for your voice to come into it, cuckoo.
In this jewelry-box deposit the long necklace of your cries
whose lost clasp keeps us busy. What a pity!

(Après-Fuite)

On aurait voulu à jamais
après ta fuite ingrate
garder ton charme secret!
Mais quelque jour on constate
que la terre se tait.

Quel mystère peureux
nous a privés de ta fête?
Même quand tu passais distraite,
tu nous rendais heureux.

Sainte-Catherine

La sainte, en montrant, acquisition trop pure,
à tout jamais la roue de sa torture
entre ses bras si doux, apprivoisée,
quelle joie dut-elle éprouver
en voyant, infiniment, la somme
de cet objet terrible comme un homme,
appartenir à sa virginité.

Elle et l'instrument qui tue et venge
s'entrepénètrent, s'aiment, ô mélange
que nul poète n'a osé inventer.
Comment sut-elle la cruelle chose,
ronde rosace avant d'être rose,
en son fécond triomphe implanter?

La voilà heureuse comme l'enfant
qui son jouet le plus aimé embrasse.
Cassée par lui, elle se rend tenace
pour être de sa roue un doux fragment.

(After-Flight)

After your thankless flight,
we'd have wanted to keep
your charm a secret forever!
But one day we realized
that the earth was keeping quiet.

What fearful mystery
deprived us of your feast?
Even when you ignored us,
you made us happy.

Saint Catherine

Forever revealing the wheel
of her torture, too pure possession,
so soft and tamed in her arms,
what joy this saint must have felt
as she saw the burden of that
terrible object like a man who
belonged to her virginity forever.

She and the instrument of death and revenge
interpenetrate and love one another, O melange
no poet ever dared to invent.
How did she know how to implant
that cruel thing—round rose-window before
being rose—in her own fertile triumph?

See, now she's as happy as a child
embracing her favorite toy.
Broken by it, she becomes tenacious
to be a tender fragment of its wheel.

(La Balle)

En attendant la balle qui retombe,
ses mains avaient un geste de colombes—
ô cœur trahi dans nos beaux jeux confus;
sans se montrer tout était manifeste,
telle impatience mêlée à tel geste
qu'arrêta tel souvenir de l'institut.

Que l'on était distrait et dans l'attente;
on provoquait la brouille, la tourmente
tant était long ce temps des doubles jeux.
Ça semblait un moment avant tant d'autres,
et c'était tout, mon Dieu, et tellement notre
et c'était trop et nous étions trop peu!

(Menace)

Que nous veut-elle, la vie dont chaque moment mortel
nous menace de mort . . . comme David mettant à sa fronde
une belle pierre blanche et ronde
pour la lancer contre l'énorme géant, le monde,
debout dans notre œil temporel?

Que nous veut-elle, qui nous fait partager avec tant
d'êtres le clair affront et l'aveugle chance?
Et qui en voulant nous aider nous étonne encore en changeant
le tissu de nos torts (que nous tourmentons) en un inextricable
    filet d'innocence?

(The Ball)

While waiting for the falling ball,
his hands were the movements of doves—
O heart betrayed in our lovely mixed-up games;
without showing itself, all was quite obvious,
some impatience mingled with some gesture
stopped by some memory of the school.

How inattentive and expectant we were;
those games of doubles lasted so long,
we provoked estrangement and torment.
It seemed a moment before so many others,
and it was all, my God, and it was so much ours,
and it was so much more and we were so much less!

(Menace)

What does she want from us, life whose every mortal moment
menaces us with death . . . like David loading his sling
with a lovely white and round stone
to launch it at the enormous giant, the world,
standing in our temporal eye?

What does she want from us, she who makes us share
the clear insult and blind chance with so many others?
And who, wanting to help us, astounds us again by changing
our faults' tissue (that we torment) into an inextricable
        thread of innocence?

(Musique)

Prends-moi par la main,
c'est pour toi si facile,
Ange, tu es le chemin
même en étant immobile.

J'ai peur, vois-tu, que personne
ici ne me cherche davantage;
moi, de ce que l'on donne,
je n'ai pu en faire usage,

alors ils m'ont délaissé.
D'abord la solitude
m'a charmé comme un prélude,
mais tant de musique m'a blessé.

Migration des Forces

Souvent devant les dévots se vide un masque
et l'idole s'excuse soudain
de son trône trompeur, de son faste fantasque,
de son or criard et commun.

Certains de nos dieux s'épuisent et se dessèchent,
arides, ankylosés;
dans d'autres, en murmurant, se jette la source fraîche
d'une divinité reposée.

(Music)

Take me by the hand,
it's so easy for you, Angel,
for you are the road
even while being immobile.

You see, I'm scared no one
here will look for me again;
I couldn't make use of
whatever was given,

so they abandoned me.
At first the solitude
charmed me like a prelude,
but so much music wounded me.

The Migration of Powers

Often a mask empties itself before believers
and suddenly the idol apologizes
for its deceitful throne, for its fantastic pomp,
for its shrill and common gold.

Some of our gods become exhausted and withered,
arid and stiff;
into others, while murmuring, tumbles the fresh spring
of a refreshed divinity.

(Nuages)

Ces ouvriers de la pluie, ces lourds nuages, voici
que le soir les rend à de célestes vacances;
un délire d'inutilité les a pris
et leur bord congédié ose des transparences.

Ils imitent nonchalamment montagnes et îles
et proposent des caps lumineux aux naufrages du regard.
Et combien, devant la lune, plus tard
deviendront féminins leurs profiles.

Autour d'eux pâlissent ces profondeurs qui tantôt
devront contenir les mondes innombrables.
Une amie qui mal se surveille dit: Beau,
et se ferme sur l'inénarrable.

(Un Saint-Esprit)

J'ai trouvé un Saint-Esprit fort défait
derrière l'autel de la chapelle;
il n'avait point péri par méfait,
mais par cette éternelle

perte des choses qui nous surprend
de sa force singulière;
du reste, il l'avoue, c'est bien navrant
que de rendre l'absence mère.

(Clouds)

These laborers of rain, these heavy clouds,
see how evening takes them on celestial vacations;
a delirium of uselessness has gripped them,
and their vacationing edges dare transparencies.

They nonchalantly imitate mountains and islands
and propose luminous caps to the shipwrecks of sight.
And later, in front of the moon,
how many of their profiles will become feminine.

Around them, these depths which soon
ought to hold the numberless worlds, blanch.
And a friend who doesn't watch herself says: Nice,
and closes herself on the unutterable.

(Holy Ghost)

Behind the altar in the chapel
I found a demolished Holy Ghost;
he hadn't perished from wrongdoing,
but, instead, from that eternal

loss of things that surprises us
with its inimitable powers;
the rest, he admits, is as harrowing
as making absence into mother.

(Grisaille)

La vigne fait tant de vrilles
qui ne trouvent pas d'appui;
mais pendant que son suc se distille,
ce sont bien celles-ci

qui ajoutent à la grisaille
(pour que l'origine soit sûre)
la légère signature
de la joie qui travaille.

(Fleur Pensive)

Parfois une fleur devenue pensive
nous reconnaît
et nous poursuit d'une attention qu'on dirait
presque auditive.

On dirait qu'elle connaît nos pas
qui s'approchent, qui passent—
elle qui passe sur place
s'étonne-t-elle de l'audace
de celui qui s'en va?

(Il Ne Se Repose Jamais)

Parmi nous il ne se repose jamais,
car en chaque mouvement que notre cœur fait
il devine et reconnaît
l'insuffisance.

Parmi les anges il ne trouve non plus de repos,
car ils murmurent toujours comme l'eau
par abondance.

(Grisaille)

The vine grows so many tendrils
that find no place to lean;
but while its sugar distills,
these are the very ones

who add to the grisaille
(so that its origin is clear)
the light signature
of the joy that is at work.

(Pensive Flower)

Sometimes, becoming pensive, a flower
recognizes us
and pursues us with attention that is
almost audible.

It's as if she knows our footsteps
approaching, leaving—
she who vanishes on the spot,
is she amazed by the audacity
of one who takes his leave?

(He Can Find No Rest)

He can find no rest among us,
for in every movement our heart makes
he predicts and recognizes
the insufficiency.

He finds no rest among the angels, either,
for they are always murmuring like water
with abundance.

Cimetière à Ragaz

C'est de ton repos inconnu
que cette douceur se dégage,
de ta jeunesse sans âge
de ton beau ciel non-su.

Ces croix aux épaules féminines
d'un élan bénévole
dressent leur bleue échine
comme des filles à l'école.

Elles t'apprennent par cœur
oubliant leur petite morte.
C'est toi ici la plus forte
qui rends distraites les fleurs.

(Grand Cœur Écouteux)

Une fois encore te voir tel
que tu étais aux yeux de mon enfance:
ô apparition des apparences,
ô bel été sucré et substanciel.

Que tu étais entier et éperdu,
tout plein, avec des papillons pour routes.
Ô nostalgie de ce pur superflu
d'un grand cœur écouteux que l'on écoute.

Cemetery in Ragaz

This escaping mildness
is from your unknown rest,
your ageless youth,
your lovely not-known sky.

These crosses with feminine shoulders
straighten their blue backbone
with an indulgent impulse
like young girls in school.

Forgetting their small dead friend,
they learn you all by heart.
Here, you are the strongest one
who makes the flowers listless.

(Great Indulgent Heart)

To see you one more time again
just as you were to my childhood eyes:
O apparition of appearances,
O lovely, sweet, sky-substanced summer.

How you were complete and wild,
completely full, with butterflies for paths.
O nostalgia for this pure excess
of a great indulgent heart that we indulge.

(Rose)

Si la rose voulait nous dire comment
elle fait pour ne pas se distraire.
Puisse ainsi l'amie à l'amant
être rose entière.

Celle qui infiniment se contient
sous des surfaces tendres
pour qu'un beau bonheur ovidien.

(Trompettes)

Comme les trompettes, jadis, renversèrent, sonnante tempête,
de la ville assiégée tourelles et remparts,
ainsi vous bâtîtes en moi, orgues concrètes,
l'ineffable cité sous un ciel d'étendards.

Il se dresse, mon cœur, avec ses tours, ses murailles,
et comme dans d'anciens parchemins peints,
moi, qui l'habite debout, je suis à sa taille,
aussi haut que ma ville et fort de son être soudain.

(Des Adieux, Encore des Adieux)

Des adieux, encore des adieux!
Ô mes amis, jouissons mieux
de ce beau bonheur d'être ceux
qui parfois s'entrearrêtent.
Reste, ne t'en vas pas encore,
ne sois pas ce presque-mort
que boit la distance distraite.

(Rose)

If only the rose wished to tell us
what she does to concentrate.
Likewise, the lover's friend
could be entirely rose.

She who contains herself forever
under tender surfaces
for one handsome ovidian joy.

(Trumpets)

Just as the trumpets' ringing tempest once toppled
the turrets and ramparts of besieged cities,
so too, concrete organs, have you erected in me
the ineffable city under a sky of barriers.

My heart rises with these towers, these high walls,
and, as in ancient painted parchments,
I, who inhabit it standing, I am at its side,
as high as my city and strong with its sudden being.

(Goodbyes, Still More Goodbyes)

Goodbyes, still more goodbyes!
O my friends, let us revel longer
in the lovely joy of being those
who sometimes stopped each other.
Stay, don't leave quite yet,
don't be the nearly dead
that inattentive distance drinks.

Puisqu'on ne pénètre jamais
là où chacun refait
son risqué royaume,
l'on se trouve ainsi à mi-chemin
entre les cœurs voisins
sur le carrefour des paumes.

(Soliste)

En musique seulement il y a de semblables surprises
quand au milieu d'une phrase trop indécise
monte le brusque sanglot d'un violon.
Ainsi dans un chant longtemps chargé de vie triste,
il se fit une place pour l'abandon
dont mon cœur était le soliste.

(Rose le Dimanche)

De toujours vous voir ainsi sur ce travail qui vous penche
et autour de vous cette perte,
comment ne pas vous jeter par la fenêtre ouverte
d'une rose le dimanche?

Voyez-vous c'est tout un mois de pétales: aucun
d'aucun devoir ne porte la marque quelconque.
D'un tendre cœur qu'aucune force ne tronque:
quel calepin!

Since we never penetrate
that place where each remakes
the kingdom that was risked,
we thus find ourselves halfway
between neighboring hearts
in the public square of palms.

(Soloist)

Only in music are there similar surprises
when, in the middle of too vague a phrase,
the brusque sob of a violin rises.
So in a song long burdened by a paltry life,
there was one place of abandonment
for which my heart was soloist.

(Rose on Sunday)

To see you always bent over that work
and this loss all around you,
how could I not toss a rose
through the open window on Sunday?

See, it's a whole month of petals:
not one exercise bears a mediocre grade.
From a tender heart no power can cut short:
what a workbook!

(Écart)

Nous savions tout cela avant ta venue tendre,
doux printemps infini.
Car rien qu'à deviner: un bonheur est à vendre ...
déjà on donne le prix.

Déjà, mon Dieu, déjà, la vie se précipite
vers cet abîme de vie.
Et cet écart déjà de la parole dite
qui déjà nous renie. . . .

(Feu d'Automne)

Quel beau feu clair
vous avez allumé au carrefour de ma vie,
quel beau feu clair.
Et comme sa pure force assouvie
fait trembler l'air!

Clarté qui tremble de ce feu d'automne
pour être humainement
plus près de nous, plus émue et plus bonne
en ressemblant au temps.

[Lausanne, septembre 1926]

(Loss)

We knew all that before your tender coming,
sweet infinite spring.
For it's nothing to divine: a blessing's up for sale ...
we already pay the price.

Already, God, already life hurls itself
toward this abyss of life.
And already this loss of the spoken word
that already denies us. . . .

(Autumn Fire)

What a lovely, brilliant fire
you lit at the crossroads of my life,
such a lovely, brilliant fire.
And how its pure, satiated power
makes the air tremble!

Light trembling with this autumn fire
to be humanly
closer to us, more moving, and better
by resembling the season.

[Lausanne, September 1926]

Dédicaces et Fragments

Dedications and Fragments

Dédicaces

À MONIQUE ET BLAISE BRIOD

Et à la lampe et à votre feu
ces grandes pages seront familières;
si de comprendre vous fatigue un peu,
tenez les simplement à la lumière
qu'elle les dore à son gré.
Ces grandes pages aiment à se taire:
Tant de silence y a collaboré.

À PIA DI VALMARANA

Si la langue ne tout vous retient,
si un peu de moi se précise,
rendez à l'air de Venise
un peu de mon cœur *vénitien*.

Il le fut à combien d'heures
doucement initié,
et croyez qu'il le demeure,
même éloigné. . . .

À MISS NICOLA B.

Comme tel dessin de maître accapare
le vide du papier entre les traits,
tant que son blanc paraît précieux et rare,
ainsi décide le dessin parfait

de tes sourcils et de ta bouche pure
de ces distances et de la matière
qui entre ton menton et tes paupières
se vantent, belle, d'être ta figure.

Dedications

TO MONIQUE AND BLAISE BRIOD

And by your fire and by lamplight
these big pages will become familiar;
if understanding tires you a bit,
simply hold them to the light
to gild them at its pleasure.
These big pages love to be quiet:
So much silence has collaborated here.

TO PIA DI VALMARANA

If the tongue keeps nothing from you,
if a little of me becomes clear,
to the air of Venice offer
a bit of my Venetian heart.

It was gently initiated there
during so many hours
and, believe me, it remains there,
even from afar. . . .

TO MISS NICOLA B.

Just as the master's drawing hoards
the paper's emptiness between its strokes,
its white seems so rare and precious,
so too the perfect structure of your eyebrows

and of your pure mouth determines
the spaces and substances
which, between your eyelids and your chin,
lovely woman, are proud to be your face.

À MADAME LA BARONNE
RENÉE DE BRIMONT

Pour trouver Dieu il faut être heureux
car ceux qui par détresse l'inventent
vont trop vite et cherchent trop peu
l'intimité de son absence ardente.

À MARIE LAURENCIN

Comme dans les cartes de géographie
les points indiquent des villes,
ainsi (à mille
lieues d'ici)
leurs yeux sont habités. . . .

Et de leurs corps les contours mouvants
aux frontières discrètes
chantent le tendre changement
d'innombrables conquêtes
sans conquérant.

BELLA:

en somme elle y est trop peu,
mais vous la retrouverez encore.
Si vous y voyez sa mort,
un ruban d'elle, de ses cheveux
une mèche, de son blond feu
un reflet, voire de son corps
la flottante chaleur: tout cela
dans d'autres pages vous surprendra
comme un tendre aveu
posthume. . . .

TO MADAME THE BARONESS
RENÉE DE BRIMONT

One must be happy to find God
for those who invent him out of grief
move too fast and search too little
for the intimacy of his ardent absence.

TO MARIE LAURENCIN

Just as on maps
dots are signs of cities,
so (a thousand
leagues from here)
their eyes are occupied....

And at discreet frontiers
their bodies' moving outlines
sing the gentle change
of numberless conquests
without conquering.

BELLA:

in short, she is not enough,
but you will rediscover her again.
If you should see her death,
one of her ribbons, a wisp
of her hair, the glint of her
blonde fire, see the floating
warmth of her body: all that,
in other pages, will surprise you
like a tender, posthumous
acknowledgment....

À MADEMOISELLE SOPHY GIAUQUE

C'est notre extrême labeur:
de trouver une écriture
qui résiste aux pleurs
et qui devant nous re-figure,
précis dans leur clarté pure,
les beaux adieux navigateurs.

À NATALIE CLIFFORD-BARNEY

Ô le temple défait ou jamais terminé! Comment
adorer un Dieu qui tant se plaît aux ruines!

Les offrandes usent l'autel et le sel de nos larmes marines
ronge les dalles. Et quant aux colonnes: à deux
on les soutient; c'est leur beau fût qui sépare
les amants.... Aussi l'entraînent-ils avec eux
dans la lente chute de leurs étreintes avares.

À MARINA ZWETAJEWA-EFRON

Marina: voici galets et coquillages
ramassés récemment à la française plage
de mon étrange cœur.... (J'aimerais que tu connusses
toutes les étendues de son divers paysage,
depuis sa côte bleue jusqu'à ses plaines russes.)

TO MADEMOISELLE SOPHY GIAUQUE

This is our utmost task:
to find a literature
that can resist our tears
and which before us re-imagines,
precise in their pure clarity,
beautiful seafaring goodbyes.

TO NATALIE CLIFFORD-BARNEY

O the destroyed or never finished temple! How
can we adore a God who takes such pleasure in ruins!

The offerings wear the altar down and the salt of our sea-tears
gnaws at the flagstones. As for the columns: it takes two
of us to hold them up; it's their handsome shaft that separates
lovers. . . . And they drag lovers down with them
in the slow collapse of their avaricious embrace.

TO MARINA ZWETAJEWA-EFRON

Marina: here are shells and pebbles
recently gathered from the French beach
of my stranger's heart. . . . (I'd like you to know
all the expanses of its divers landscape,
from its azure coast to its Russian plains.)

À MADAME JEANNE-RENÉE DUBOST

Ô le ruban léger dont les bouts flottent,
poème sur un thème éternel
qu'écrit soudain un doux vent polyglotte,
qui te lirait selon ton sens réel,
flottant adieu, qu'attendrait-il encore
de cette vie à l'abandon fatal,
où parfois un jardin hivernal
rend apparente la statue d'une Flore....

À ISABELLE TRUMPY

À ces moments si beaux
avant les paroles et entre ...
(chacun si près de ce centre
où il faut à peine des mots),

   à la robe couleur de roseaux
   qui chantait la mélopée verte
   en y ajoutant (sage! ô!)
   le pur noir de nos pertes.

     À vous qui sembliez votre sœur
     pour être vous davantage!
      À la magie des images
      en ce monde évocateur!

À MIMI ROMANELLI

Qu'il nous soit permis de temps en temps
de pleurer et de rêver sur un livre,
mais s'ouvrir grandement quand même: c'est vivre,
pour *être lu* de Dieu qui nous comprend.

TO MADAME JEANNE-RENÉE DUBOST

Oh, a thin ribbon with streaming ends,
poem on an eternal theme
suddenly written by a polyglot wind,
who will read your real meaning,
streaming goodbye, who will still hear
you in this life of fatal abandon,
where sometimes a winter garden
reveals a statue of Flora. . . .

TO ISABELLE TRUMPY

To these lovely moments
before and between words. . .
(each so near the center
where words are barely needed),

to the reed-colored dress
singing the green recitative
and adding to it (oh! wise!)
the pure black of our losses.

To you who seem to be your sister
to be that much more yourself!
To the magic of images
in this evocative world!

TO MIMI ROMANELLI

From time to time, let us be allowed
to weep and dream over a book,
and yet leave ourselves completely open: living
is *to be read* by God who comprehends us.

POUR SERVIR D'ÉPITAPHE
À LA BELLE MADAME B . . .

Que j'étais belle! Ce que je vois
me fait penser à ma beauté, ô Maître!
Ce ciel, tes Anges—mais c'était moi,
l'étonnement en plus de ne pas l'être.

À ODILON-JEAN PÉRIER

Nos anges, Monsieur, se sont bien reconnus,
ils n'étaient pas à leur première rencontre;
ne l'oubliez pas: ne portant pas de montre,
ils avancent toujours sur tout temps prévu.

À JEAN-LOUIS VAUDOYER

> *«À cette époque, Aubanel ne sait pas*
> *qu'il aime,* qu'il aimera bientôt. . . . »*

C'est déjà trop osé, quand il faut dire: j'aime.
C'est un trop brusque fait qui démolit les mots.
Ne serait-ce de nos cœurs la faculté extrême
de chanter: je suis seul, mais j'aimerai bientôt?

Car dire: j'ai aimé . . . hélas, les pleurs s'y mêlent.
C'est une de nos fleurs emportée par les eaux.
Si debout qu'elle soit, d'ériger une stèle,
c'est obéir à un tombeau. . . .

TO SERVE AS AN EPITAPH
FOR THE BEAUTIFUL MADAME B . . .

How beautiful I was! Everything I see,
my Lord, reminds me of my beauty!
This paradise, your Angels—but they were me,
still greater astonishment of not being me.

TO ODILON-JEAN PÉRIER

Our angels, sir, surely recognized each other,
that was not the first time that they met;
do not forget: since they don't wear a watch,
they always travel on foreshadowed time.

TO JEAN-LOUIS VAUDOYER

> "At this time, Aubanel does not know
> that he loves, that soon he'll be in love. . . ."

It's already too much when we must say: I love.
It's too brusque a fact that demolishes the words.
Should it not be our heart's greatest faculty
to sing: I am alone, but soon I'll be in love?

Because to say: I loved . . . ah, there are tears in that.
That is one of our flowers brought by the waters.
However upright it may be, to erect a stele
is to obey a tomb. . . .

À NIGROVORINE QUI S'EN VA

Tu fais «non» de ton corps, et *non,*
comme on fait *non* de la tête.
Pour entendre si l'on répond,
parfois tu t'arrêtes.

Tu te consumes, petite martyre,
grise dévote;
pour qu'elle expire
tu frottes la faute!

En sa plus secrète nature
tu l'irrites et tu l'agaces,
et tu mets à sa place
la pure fin de ta trace pure.

À M...

Les autres, c'était la tempête,
la haine d'amour, le remous.
Toi seule, tu prenais ma tête
et, la mettant sur tes genoux,
tu disais: mon ami, pleure,
je mettrai mes mains apaisées
dans tes cheveux. C'est l'heure:
car moi, j'ai déjà pleuré....

TO NIGROVORINE WHO IS LEAVING

You say "no" with your body, and *no*
as one who says *no* with her head.
Now and then you stop yourself
to hear whether we answer.

You consume yourself, little martyr,
excited devotee;
you rub the error
so that it will vanish!

You irritate and aggravate it
in its most secret nature,
leaving in its place
the pure end of your pure trace.

TO M . . .

The others were the tempest,
love's hatred, the whirlpool.
You alone, you took my head
and, placing it on your knees,
you said: my friend, weep,
I'll place my appeased hands
in your hair. It's time:
for I, I have already wept. . . .

À BETSY STEIGER

Les feuilles tombent, tombent. . . .
Et c'est notre pas qui les mêle
à la terre. Elles succombent.
Mais si ton cœur, Betsy, tombe,
il se laisse tomber sur ses ailes:
cette feuille est une colombe.
Cette colombe qui semble
tomber est un «cœur attentif» . . .
un cœur tendre et vif
d'une colombe qui tremble.
Mais qui reprendra son vol
vers une clarté ouverte,
tandis que les feuilles inertes
rentreront dans le sol.

TO BETSY STEIGER

The leaves fall, fall. . . .
And it's our step that mixes them
with the earth. They succumb.
But, Betsy, if your heart falls,
it lets itself fall on its wings:
that leaf is a dove.
The dove seems to be
falling as an "attentive heart" . . .
the tender and quick heart
of a trembling dove.
But it will take flight again
toward an open brightness,
while the inert leaves
will go back into the ground.

Fragments

Ô source qui jaillit, ô volonté secrète
de vivre parmi nous et d'être de nos pleurs!
Vive divinité et transparente bête,
amante du départ, distraite sœur....

(«Autre Source»)

Multiple chant, qui rend à nos oreilles
l'équivalent, sans perte, d'un chemin....

(Pour une autre «Source»)

Et la beauté devient toujours plus difficile,
c'était d'abord le geste quotidien....

Moines énormes et forts qui de leur place
tenaient l'éternité, le ciel en fleur
famille d'acier et d'or, tenace race
qui invinciblement de son ardeur
dressait des monastères comme des menaces....

Non je ne veux plus: non,
de cette suprême aurore
comment pourrais-je encore
survivre à l'abandon....

L'amour, je le sais, c'est une perte
cachée par un geste qui prend.
Ô mes tiges vertes,
rendez mes fleurs inertes
et fermez-les lentement....

Fragments

Onrushing spring, O secret will
to live among us and to be our tears!
Bright divinity and transparent beast,
lover of departure, listless sister. . . .

("Another Spring")

⌐

Multiple song that carries to our ears
the equivalent of a road with no loss. . . .

(For another "Spring")

⌐

And beauty becomes ever more difficult,
once it was a daily gesture. . . .

⌐

Enormous and strong monks who from their place
maintained eternity, heaven in bloom,
family of steel and gold, tenacious race
which with its fervent zeal invincibly
erected monasteries like menaces. . . .

⌐

No, I want no more: no,
after this amazing dawn
how could I possibly
survive abandon again. . . .

⌐

Love, I know, is a loss
hidden by an act that roots.
O my green stems,
make my flowers quite inert
and, slowly, close them up. . . .

⌐

Ô vie vécue depuis quel temps! Ô vie
qui s'adonnait subtilisant ces bouches
et qui enfin les laisse sans retouche. . . .

⁓

Voilà la nuit t'ouvrant ses bras d'espace.
Vas-y te blottir comme un jeune amant,
ferme les yeux à ce moindre vent
et tu auras sa face sur ta face. . . .

⁓

A force de prier il se fait un archange. . . .

⁓

Tout épris d'avenir, je contemple les cieux. . . .

⁓

Où je ne voulais que chanter,
il m'a été accordé
l'honneur de la vie. . . .

⁓

Roi: l'homme qui un instant
s'arrête sous une couronne,
toit qui attire la foudre. . . .

⁓

Ne nommons point ce qui fut le passé,
un chemin de lumière reste tracé
dans le ciel que nous regardâmes
jadis de nos clairs yeux d'autrefois. . . .

⁓

Soudain il me souvient d'une place
auprès d'une source prise de manière
qu'un banc en pierre qui l'enlace
vous invitait à vous taire. . . .

⁓

O life lived since who knows when!
O life that got on by retouching her mouths
and at last leaves them untouched. . . .

~

See how night opens for you its arms of space.
Go curl up against it like a young lover,
close your eyes to that lesser wind
and its face will be on your face. . . .

~

By sheer dint of prayer he makes himself an archangel. . . .

~

All infatuated with the future, I contemplate the skies. . . .

~

When all I wanted was to sing,
I was accorded
the honor of living. . . .

~

King: a man who for a moment
stops himself under a crown,
a roof attracting thunderbolts. . . .

~

Let us not name what was the past,
a road of light remains still traced
across the sky we used to look at
with our eyes that once were clear. . . .

~

Suddenly I recall a place
near a well set in such a way
the stone bench surrounding it
invited you to be quiet. . . .

~

Quelle étrange passion
que celle où se transforment
tant de choses qui dorment
en des paroles qui font

un silence de fleurs...?

⁓

Peut-être que je trouve mon amante
toute éplorée à l'ombre de mon sang....

⁓

Au lieu de cette vie où l'on demeure
tout rapproché et pourtant mal uni,
au lieu de cette chance que l'on pleure,
nous aurons eu peut-être une heure
et toute la durée en raccourci....

⁓

Qu'on ne s'obstine pas, car tout nous montre
l'infinité de l'instant accepté....

⁓

Le moine s'y renferme, pour que son dieu
le trouve à l'endroit convenu;
quant au prisonnier, on ne le cherche plus,
il n'y a pas de dieux curieux....

*(«Ce Soir Quelque Chose
sans l'Air A Passé...»)*

⁓

Le soir, chez elle soulevée
dans sa chambre claire et tranquille,
c'est son simple cœur qui rend la ville
à la nuit démesurée....

⁓

What stranger passion
than that in which so many
sleeping things transform themselves
into words that make

a silence of flowers. . . ?

⁓

Perhaps I'll find my lover
all in tears in the shadow of my blood. . . .

⁓

Instead of this life in which we remain
all very close yet poorly matched,
instead of this fate we lament,
perhaps we might have had one hour
and the whole duration shortened. . . .

⁓

Let's not be obstinate, for all reveals
the infinity of the accepted moment. . . .

⁓

The monk locks himself up so that his god
will find him in the stipulated place;
the prisoner's not hunted anymore,
he doesn't have such curious gods. . . .

("Tonight There Was
Something in the Air. . .")

⁓

At night, back upstairs
in her bright and quiet room,
her simple heart returns the town
to the unbounded night. . . .

⁓

On fait à la terre une nouvelle surface;
une couche innocente remplace
celle qui du sort fut touchée. . . .

～

Profond amour qui de la terre s'élève. . . .

～

Viens admirer cette heure qui s'argente,
s'adoucissant après une journée d'or. . . .

～

Si nous sentions un seul jour
ce que c'est que le pain. . . .

～

Comme la nuit la rendait incertaine
dans sa robe blanche qui à peine
semblait aussi claire, aussi pleine
qu'un rayon de lune que personne
ne saurait porter ou habiter. . . .

～

Tout ce qui fut divin, reste divin.
Jamais le ciel ne perd une couronne.
Grande, assise, la déesse donne
aux dieux futurs la source de son sein. . . .

～

Il faut, mon cœur, abdiquer de l'attente. . . .

～

À moins que ce soit
une chapelle fruste
qui montre son humble toit
et le portique vétuste. . . .

(«Chemins Qui Se Menent Nulle Part»)

～

We have made a new surface of the earth;
an innocent childbirth replaces
the one that had been touched by fate. . . .

꙳

Profound lover rising from the earth. . . .

꙳

Come admire this hour turning silver,
softening itself after a whole day of gold. . . .

꙳

If for just one day we knew
only what bread is. . . .

꙳

How the night made her uncertain
in her white dress that seemed
just as bright and just as full
as a ray of moonlight no one
would know how to carry or to wear. . . .

꙳

All that was divine remains divine.
Heaven won't lose one crown.
Seated, grand, the goddess gives
future gods the power of her breast. . . .

꙳

My heart, we must abdicate this waiting. . . .

꙳

At least let it be
a dilapidated chapel
with a humble roof
and a decaying door. . . .

("Roads Leading Nowhere")

꙳

Si la mort était un mal, nous serions entourés
d'animaux affolés. . . .

⁓

Ô moment, entre tous inconcevable,
quand le sourire de l'amie, l'instable
sourire, ne semble plus attaché à sa face
avant d'appartenir encore à l'espace
dont il sera. . . .

⁓

Le vent de quel souvenir, de quelle vie le vent
a posé en passant un masque sur mon être. . . .

⁓

La perte brusque peut être cruelle, mais l'autre,
celle qui fait qu'une chose infiniment nôtre. . . .

⁓

Les Dieux: ces obstinés qui vivent
du démenti. . . .

⁓

Les longs adieux des nénuphars mourants
ont-ils assez duré pour cette sainte
ouïe de votre œil? Qu'un autre chant,
montant celui-ci, remplace leur complainte
d'un blanc majeur. . . .

⁓

Divinité du sommeil des chats,
sous un ciel sans fentes,
j'aurais été celui qui édifia
ton temple aux voûtes lentes. . . .

⁓

If death were something evil, we'd be surrounded
by demented animals. . . .

O moment, inconceivable to all,
when a friend's smile, an unstable
smile, no longer seems attached to her face
before again belonging to the space
that it will be. . . .

The wind of what memory, from what life did the wind
in passing deposit a mask on my being. . . .

A sudden loss can be cruel, but that other,
the one making one thing infinitely ours. . . .

The Gods: those obstinates who live
on contradiction. . . .

Did the long goodbyes of dying water lilies
last long enough for that holy
hearing of your eye? May another song,
rising even higher, replace their complaint
in white major. . . .

Divinity of the sleep of cats,
under an unbroken sky,
I would have been the one erecting
your temple of slow vaults. . . .

Le jour est incertain, la nuit est éphémère.
C'est le poète qui les rend à Dieu.
Ni plus connus, ni moins douloureux:
un peu plus commencés et tout à faire.…

⁓

Quelque lenteur qui traversait le jour:
on aurait dit l'enterrement des rêves.…

⁓

N'oublie pas, étranger, de faire tes adieux
à l'heure infinie où tout te tient et t'aime.…

⁓

Est-ce des Dieux en fuite
que résonne le sol.…

⁓

«chapiteaux peuris d'acanthes corinthiennes»
Moment où il faudrait dire un mot en acanthe,
un de ces mots qui terminent une colonne qui vante
sa vigueur de porter, sa montée lente
vers cette feuillaison.…

⁓

On voudrait un peu de clémence, un peu
de cet entre-deux unique
qui semble comme un aveu
de la musique
de ne pouvoir rien sur le silence.…

⁓

Day is uncertain, night is ephemeral.
The poet offers them to God.
Neither more known, nor less sorrowful:
a little more started and still everything to do. . . .

⁓

Some slowness across the day
like the burial of dreams. . . .

⁓

Stranger, don't forget to say goodbye
to that infinite hour when all holds you and loves you. . . .

⁓

Is it the flight of God
that makes the sun resound. . . .

⁓

                    "capitals in bloom with Corinthian acanthus"
Moment when we should speak an acanthus word,
one of those words which top a column that boasts
its strength to bear, its slow rise
toward these blooms of leaves. . . .

⁓

We'd want a little mercy, a little
of this unequaled interval
that seems like music's
avowal
of having no power on silence. . . .

⁓

C'est pourtant en nous, le secret de la vie
et non pas chez les Dieux
qui n'ont que des souvenirs de chasse.
C'est en nous que s'enlacent
l'ami et l'ennemi,
éperdus, silencieux. . . .

⁓

Tu as sur nous le tendre avantage
d'être tenu sans jamais te tenir,
et dans l'ancienne terre fond ton âge
et se consume pour la rajeunir. . . .

(«*Encore, Encore Je Vais et Je M'Incline* . . .»)

⁓

Astre de nos absents, ô miroir distrait
. . . ami des coquillages, des ongles et des os. . . .

⁓

Sommes-nous seuls à avoir reçu
ce bruit étrange qu'une rose fait
laissant tomber contre un marbre frais
toute sa vie, ce doux corps qu'elle était.
Vous l'avez entendu, je vous ai cru
dans mon oreille. . . . Mythe qui nous frôle,
antique aile rentrée dans l'épaule. . . .

⁓

Pourquoi a-t-on parfois l'âme si lasse
malgré ce cœur si doux?
Ceux qui chantent, hélas, et qui enchantent, passent
et la vie muette, tenace,
reste rivée contre nous. . . .

⁓

And yet life's secret is in us
and not in the Gods
who remember only the hunt.
In us the friend and enemy
intertwine,
desperate, speechless. . . .

     ⌒

You have the tender advantage over us
of being held without ever holding on,
and in the ancient earth your age melts
and burns to make it young again. . . .

                  ("Again, Again I Go and Lean . . .")

     ⌒

Star of our absent ones, O listless mirror
. . . friend of shells, of fingernails, and bones. . . .

     ⌒

Are we the only ones to have received
this strange noise made by a rose
as it lets all its life fall, this sweet body
that it was, against the cool marble.
You have heard it, I believed you
in my ear. . . . Myth brushing by us,
ancient wing entering our shoulder. . . .

     ⌒

Why is our soul sometimes so weary
despite this tender heart?
Ah, those who chant and who enchant
pass on, and life, tenacious, mute,
remains riveted against us. . . .

     ⌒

Auront le paradis ceux qui vantent les choses
car quel examen de félicité,
que de refaire avec des paroles la rose
ou d'imiter de la pomme la belle prose!
Quelle universelle complicité...!

⁓

Après une journée de pluie pratique
voici le ciel reposé qui change
en ramassant de beaux nuages bibliques,
ameublement de prophètes et d'anges.
Et d'entre eux quelle profondeur avide
d'elle-même....

⁓

Parfois tel animal de son regard t'arrête
mi-hautain, mi-timoré,
avec sur tous les plans de sa millénaire tête....

⁓

Tout nous condamne à être de cette lente
race ... âme probante....

⁓

Aimant soudain, hélas, on ne fait que changer
d'inquiétude....

⁓

Que ton absence soit une nouvelle figure
de ton être à jamais senti;
ton ineffable départ, sûre amie, inaugure
tout un art de survie....

⁓

Will those who praise things go to paradise
for no better test of worthiness
than remaking the rose with words
or imitating the apple with lovely prose!
What universal complicity...!

～

After a day of practical rain,
look how the rested sky changes
by gathering lovely biblical clouds,
the furnishings of prophets and angels.
And among them, her own avid
depth....

～

Now and then some animal stops you
with its look half-haughty, half-frightened,
the angle of his millennial head on all....

～

All condemns us to be part
of this slow race ... probing soul....

～

Ah, sudden lover, we have simply
exchanged anxieties....

～

Let your absence be the latest shape
of your being felt forever;
sure friend, your unspeakable departure
inaugurates a whole art of survival....

～

Comment te faire encore hésiter, bel été....

Vous, vous toutes qui savent bénir
peut-être malgré vous....

(Cimetière, encore, de Ragaz)

How to make you linger more, lovely summer. . . .

You, all of you who know how to bless
perhaps despite yourselves. . . .

(Cemetery in Ragaz, again)

Translator's Notes

The Roses

Most of these poems are part of Rilke's original sequence, *Les Roses.*
However, poems XXIV, XXV, and XXVI are from Rilke's notebooks
(1921–1926) where they are grouped together under the French title
«Roses.»

The Windows

The first ten of these poems were originally published in *Les Fenêtres*
(1927). Poems III, IX, and XI, however, originally had been included in
Rilke's other sequence, *Vergers,* published in 1926.

Poems XII and XIII are from Rilke's notebooks (1921–1926). While
they are ostensibly two versions of the same poem, it seems rather clear
they ultimately turned out to be two entirely different poems.

Poems XIV and XV are also from Rilke's notebooks and are preceded
by Rilke's notation, «D'Un Cycle: ‹Fenêtres›.»

Although these last four poems were excluded from the sequence
published in 1926, at one time or another they obviously were conceived
as being part of it. That is why I am including them here.

Orchards

Rilke included poems 1, 2, and 3 (the third with an additional stanza)
from "Orchards" in his sequence, "Affectionate Taxes to France."

Rilke also included the three-poem sequence, "The Window" (Poems
50, I, II, and III), from "Orchards" in the longer sequence by the same
name included in "The Windows."

About the Author

RAINER MARIA RILKE was born in Prague, Czechoslovakia, in 1875 and died in Val-Mont, Switzerland, in 1926. Between 1901 and 1915, Rilke lived in and around Paris, during which time he briefly served as Rodin's informal secretary. Befriended by such figures as Lou Andréas-Salomé and the Princess Marie von Thurn und Taxis-Hohenlohe, he traveled to Russia, Egypt, and throughout Europe. His other friends and acquaintances included Stefan George, Paul Klee, Kokoschka, Stefan Zweig, André Gide, and Paul Valéry.

Among Rilke's many books in English translation are: *Poems 1906–1926*, *The Book of Pictures*, *The Book of Hours*, *Duino Elegies*, *The Sonnets to Orpheus*, *The Notebooks of Malte Laurids Brigge*, *The Lay of the Love and Death of Cornet Christoph Rilke*, *New Poems*, and *Letters to a Young Poet*.

No book-length collection of Rilke's French poems in English translation appeared until the publication of *Saltimbanques* (limited edition, 1978), *The Roses & The Windows* (1980), *The Astonishment of Origins* (1982), *Orchards* (1982), and *The Migration of Powers* (1984), all translated by A. Poulin, Jr. and published by Graywolf Press.

All of Rainer Maria Rilke's French poems are collected in: Rainer Maria Rilke, *Sämtliche Werke*, Zweiter Band, Gedichte: Zweiter Teil, Insel-Verlag, 1958.

About the Translator

A. POULIN, JR. was born in Lisbon, Maine, in 1938, and graduated from St. Francis College, Loyola University, and the University of Iowa. He was the author of *In Advent: Poems*; *Catawba: Omens, Prayers & Songs*; *The Slaughter of Pigs*; *A Momentary Order* (Graywolf); *Cave Dwellers* (Graywolf); and most recently, *A. Poulin, Jr. Selected Poems* (BOA Editions). He was the editor of *Contemporary American Poetry*, now in its seventh edition; and his translations of Rainer Maria Rilke's *Duino Elegies* and *The Sonnets to Orpheus* were highly acclaimed. The founding editor/publisher of BOA Editions, Ltd., he was Professor of English at the State University of New York College at Brockport. Mr. Poulin died in 1996.

This book was designed by Wendy Holdman. It is set in Minion, a typeface designed by Robert Slimbach and issued by Adobe in 1989. Composed by Stanton Publication Services, Inc., and manufactured by Maple Vail Book Manufacturing on acid-free paper.